Southern
weddings

Southern weddings

New Looks from the Old South

Tara Guérard

with Holly Burns

photography by Liz Banfield

Wyrick & Company

AN IMPRINT OF GIBBS SMITH, PUBLISHER

Salt Lake City | *Charleston* | *Santa Fe* | *Santa Barbara*

First Edition

11 10 09 08 07 5 4 3 2 1

Text ©2007 Tara Guérard

Photographs © 2007 Liz Banfield except pages 166–179 © 2007 Adrienne Page

Published by

Wyrick & Company

An imprint of Gibbs Smith, Publisher

P.O. Box 667

Layton, UT 84041

Orders: 1.800.835.4993

www.gibbs-smith.com

Creative Direction: Richard Gee, Jr., Gee Creative

Design/Art Direction: Julia O'Neal Shuman

Consultant: Martha Patrick Robbins

Printed and bound in Hong Kong

Library of Congress Cataloging-in-Publication Data

Guérard, Tara.

  Southern weddings : new looks from the old south / Tara Guérard ; photographs by Liz Banfield.—1st ed.

     p. cm.

  ISBN-13: 978-0-941711-93-7

  ISBN-10: 0-941711-93-5

  1. Wedding decorations. 2. Weddings—Equipment and supplies.

  3. Weddings—Southern States—Planning. I. Title.

  TT149.G94 2006

  395.2'2—dc22

                    2006025786

COVER: *Georgia Guérard (Tara's dog) poses on a historic Charleston porch.* PAGE 1: *A bride shows off her bouquet of pink peonies, miniature calla lilies, and sweet peas.* PAGE 2–3: *Jackie and Tige Howie share a kiss during their wedding dinner.* PAGE 4: *Jenny Hackenberg Keenan waits to walk down the aisle in the parlor of Drayton Hall Plantation.* OPPOSITE: *A white lounge adorns the garden of the William Aiken House.* PAGE 8–9 (LEFT TO RIGHT): *Chef James Burns prepared pistachio encrusted duck served on a cornbread crouton. Seagrass floor ottomans atop white mohair rugs along with floor glass cylinders lit a poolside rehearsal dinner. Kathryn Koebel Donovan reflects for a moment on her wedding day.* PAGE 10: *Guests enjoy after dinner music provided by the Right On band.*

It was my intent in creating this book that you as readers might find inspiration in its pages for your own perfect day. A big thank you is owed to each of the featured brides, who trusted me, motivated me, and allowed me to execute many of my crazy ideas!

Of course, it would have been impossible for me to orchestrate any of these weddings without my devoted, professional, hard-working staff. Thank you, most especially, to Martha Patrick Robbins (my left arm!), Jason Robbins (my everything!), Heather Santucci (flower designer extraordinaire), Susan Kelly, Lindy Shealy, Caroline Mancill, and Lexi Ritsch, along with our fabulous interns; Elizabeth Reeves, Erin Foster, Elli Thomas, Mary Helen Peacock, and Tziporah Schwartz.

I'm so grateful for the help and support of Mandy and Billy Reid, Charlie Poulnot, Elizabeth Porcher Jones (the calligrapher), Kate Badger Little, my union boys Chief Buddy, William, Brad, and others!, Tracy Pelham, Mary Patrick, Jon Robbins, Cami Warren, Quin Johnson, Joel Kirven, Hillary Ingle, Aunt Terri, Mom, Chef James Burns, Tara Thigpen, and the Snyder crew.

Thank you also to Richard Gee of Gee Creative and Julia Shuman (the best graphic designers ever!),, my best friend Nicki Clendening, and all my family in Camden (my hometown) and in Charleston, S.C. And, to my husband, Russell: Thank you for all of your love and support.

island style

Lauren Carifa & Keith Hollender

Combining the natural beachside beauty of a barrier

island with a signature color palette of bright teal

and chocolate brown, this elegant wedding brought

grown-up grace and charm to this couple's favorite

vacation spot.

The Sanctuary Hotel, Kiawah Island,

COUPLING

When I first met with Lauren and Keith, high school sweethearts who had dated on-and-off in college and then rekindled their flame after graduation when they both moved to New York, it was immediately obvious how in love they were. It was also a pretty busy time for the Carifa family: while spending a romantic weekend in Stratton, Vermont, Keith had popped the question after a morning walk, while unbeknownst to Lauren, her twin brother, James, was proposing to his girlfriend as well!

Though both she and Keith grew up in New Jersey and had lived and worked in Manhattan for some time, Lauren knew immediately that she wanted to hold her wedding on Kiawah Island, twenty-five miles southwest of Charleston. Having spent every summer there since she was three, she had shared its beauty first with her family and then with Keith, who'd often join her there for vacations during their courtship. They had so many memories of the island together that it was a perfect choice.

RIGHT: *The six-tier chocolate-chip cake was created by Wedding Cakes By Jim Smeal and finished with the signature crest.* OPPOSITE, BELOW: *White letterpress programs were tied with a teal ribbon and emblazoned with the Carifa crest.*

SETTING THE SCENE: DESIGN & DÉCOR

To get some insight into the couple's tastes, I sent Lauren to Kate's Paperie in New York to pick out some paper in colors that appealed to her. We decided on a bright teal to become the foundation for our theme. For Thursday's rehearsal dinner at the Carifa's Kiawah beach house, we matched it with beautiful burgundy peonies, which we placed in tall white porcelain vases down the length of the table. Our tent, which rose over the pool, was a custom sheer white organza with teal dupioni silk edging.

For Friday night's oyster roast—a laid-back affair at Briar's Creek Golf Club, with a lowcountry buffet and a bluegrass band—we paired the signature teal with yellow; it was a combination I'd seen in the couple's apartment, so I knew they'd appreciate a little taste of home! We had vases of little yellow mums everywhere—they just say "fall" to me—that were offset beautifully by hanging lanterns.

For the wedding itself, held at the River Course on Kiawah, teal was center stage again, though this time we paired it with a rich chocolate brown, using it for everything from the sign-in book and table linens to the leather ottomans and sofas in the lounge area. Especially for Lauren, we custom-designed a reoccurring motif of interlocking Cs (for Carifa), which we incorporated into almost every aspect of the décor, including the guest-bag tags, menu cards, place cards, and even the chandeliers.

SOIRÉE STEP BY STEP:
ROSE-COVERED CURTAIN TIEBACKS

YOU WILL NEED:

Chicken Wire
Floral Oasis Bricks
Floral Wire
Roses
Cutting Shears

- Measure the area that you will want your tieback to cover. Cut the chicken wire to the appropriate length and approximately double the width.

- Wrap the oasis bricks in the chicken wire and secure edges with floral wire so the bricks do not fall out once the tieback is hanging.

- Soak the oasis covered in chicken wire in water.

- Once your oasis has soaked enough, hang the tieback using screws, nails, zip ties, ribbon, or whatever is most appropriate.

- Cut the rose stems to about 3 to 4 inches.

- Insert the rose heads into the tieback until it's full of flowers and you can no longer see any oasis or chicken wire. (This should be done the day of your event to ensure the roses will be fresh.)

SIGNATURE ELEMENTS

LINENS AND THINGS

To match the teal-and white-tent at Thursday night's dinner, I had matching linens custom-made to ensure they were a perfect complement. I also had matching chair cushions created—white with teal piping—so every simple detail matched.

LIFE'S A BEACH

To bring the sea even closer to shore, the place cards for Thursday night's dinner included a tiny seashell, which we attached with a hot-glue gun onto the teal card. In keeping with the theme, we filled huge glass cylinders with seashells and placed them around the pool.

A PERFECT MATCH

For Friday night's oyster roast, we had towers of chocolate-, white-, and teal-colored cupcakes—in three different flavors. The frosting matched our theme, but we wanted something a little more special than clear glass cake stands, so we custom-painted them the same vibrant teal as the tablecloth.

SETTING THE MOOD

Because the Friday-night party was a laid-back, down-home affair, we used teal burlap for our tablecloths and napkins instead of dupioni silk. To further accentuate the casual, light-hearted mood, we served Soirée's signature Lowcountry Lemonade—peach Schnapps and lemonade over crushed ice and mint—in Mason jars instead of traditional glasses.

BEAN THERE

I wanted to find a way to display the butler cards in a unique fashion, so I filled large glass cylinders with coffee beans, finished them with a teal ribbon bearing Lauren's emblem, and then fastened each card onto a cocktail skewer and stuck it into the beans. The dark brown color was perfect in keeping with the theme, and the scent was heavenly! I did the same with the pens for the sign-in book.

PERSONAL TOUCH

As a surprise for Lauren, I had the ribbon she carried with her bouquet embroidered with the interlocking Cs. She knew it was everywhere else, but she had no idea I was going to present her with an embroidered ribbon that she could carry down the aisle and keep forever.

LEFT: *High heels were spared from the grass and ditched in favor of teal silk slippers.* OPPOSITE, LEFT: *Lauren's favorite sugar cookies were iced with the signature motif.* OPPOSITE, RIGHT: *Sets of four embroidered cocktail napkins made darling favors for each guest.*

SOIRÉE SECRETS

PLACING YOUR ATTENDANTS

Practicality and prettiness don't have to be mutually exclusive. To make sure the bridesmaids and groomsmen were equally spaced during the ceremony, we placed flowers on the grass and reminded each person to stand in front of their marker. If you do this, choose buds big enough to be seen, and be sure they're spaced equal distances from each other; not only will the symmetry create a streamlined look when your attendants are standing up there in front of the guests, but the flowers will add far more visual appeal than just drawing Xs in the ground!

SHOE CHECK

Fact: Women wear pretty shoes to weddings. Problem: When you're holding an outdoor ceremony, whether the terrain is grass or sand, those shoes run the risk of getting dirty. Solution: create a shoe check, so guests don't have to worry about ruining their best stilettos or mules. We bought tons of teal silk slippers from New York's Chinatown and placed them in huge chocolate wicker baskets at the entrance to the ceremony so guests could exchange their fancy footwear for something a little more forgiving. It's best to overestimate how many you'll need. The idea was so popular that every single pair was gone by the end of the night!

HEMSTITCHED NAPKINS

It's often worth it to spend a little more money on something you're going to be able to use for the rest of your life. For the reception dinner, we chose linen hemstitched napkins with the signature Carifa motif embroidered on them in teal. Not only were they a hit on the day itself, but now Lauren and Keith can relive their wedding memories every time they hold a dinner party!

SIGNATURE COOKIES

If you're holding your wedding somewhere besides where you live (or simply out of town), it's always nice to bring a little piece of your hometown into your special day. I called the company in New Jersey that made Lauren's favorite sugar cookies and ordered them for the reception—complete with her signature emblem frosted in teal, of course! Any couple can have a sweet treat at their wedding; why not make it a meaningful one?

PRINTS CHARMING

The designers at The Lettered Olive, our sister division of Soirée, used the patterned teal paper Lauren had selected from Kate's Paperie to line the inside of the save-the-date cards; we also included a poignant and funny poem about how the couple had first met. For the rehearsal dinner, we had a calligrapher hand-write each invitation and place card; they were teal with white writing, and the menu cards were complementary. We used our motif of intertwined Cs on everything for the wedding—invitations, programs, menu cards, butler cards, place cards, even our guest-bag tags—using teal and chocolate brown throughout. The menu card served a dual purpose: the name of each guest was written on the front and placed at the table; when the teal ribbon was untied, the card opened to reveal the menu.

HAPPY ENDINGS

Lauren and Keith left the reception—with the band following them, playing "When the Saints Go Marching In"—and hopped into a vintage Rolls Royce that we'd decorated with a white rose wreath on the front and a "Just Married" sign in scrollwork on the back. Once Lauren was safely ensconced in the back of the car, her father leaned in and handed her a letter through the window. "It contained everything he wanted to say to me but couldn't, because he knew it would make him cry," she told me. "I read it in the back of the car before we drove away from the reception, and it was truly a perfect moment."

RIGHT: *At each place setting, a
chocolate brown package
opened to reveal the menu.*

modern tradition

Amy Baker & Andrew Fried

A couple's keen sense of their Jewish heritage—as well

as the bride's desire to showcase her Southern roots in

a personalized, welcoming way—gave rise to a modish

fall wedding, rich with opulent hues and fanciful,

contemporary touches.

THE WEDDING CEREMONY
OF

amy rona baker
TO
andrew harris fried

SATURDAY, THE SIXTEENTH OF OCTOBE
TWO THOUSAND AND FOUR
AT HALF PAST SIX O'CLOCK

THE WILLIAM AIKEN HOUSE
CHARLESTON, SOUTH CAROLINA

COUPLING

Although Amy grew up in Charleston, she'd lived in New York for some time before she met Andrew, a native of the Big Apple. He was finishing up his first year of law school in Boston when Amy happened to come up from Manhattan for a conference. A mutual friend suggested they all meet for drinks, though, says Andrew, "He kept stressing that it wasn't a set-up!"

Something must have clicked, as a month later, when Andrew was in Manhattan, he got in touch with Amy and suggested they meet again. After a year and a half of dating—during which Andrew made frequent trips back and forth from Boston, eventually moving to New York for good—the couple got engaged that December. I met with them shortly afterwards, when they were back in Charleston for the holidays, visiting Amy's family. Soirée's offices are right around the corner from Amy's childhood home, which lent a lovely sense of familiarity to the whole process.

RIGHT: *A separate, smaller tent provided a place to lounge after dinner on velvet-covered Indian sofas.* OPPOSITE, BELOW: *Baskets of square-shaped ceremony programs also contained deep orangey-red yarmulkes for Jewish male guests to don during the traditional ceremony.*

ABOVE, LEFT: *Trays of lentils wrapped with silk ribbons made for pretty and practical décor.* ABOVE, RIGHT: *Square chargers and square centerpieces complemented square tables, dressed with lush orange.*

SETTING THE SCENE: DESIGN & DÉCOR

Because the couple wanted a fall wedding, we immediately decided on a color palette of deep oranges and reds. We paired them with rich, lush fabrics—raw silks and velvets, which appeared in every detail—to add to that sumptuous, autumnal feel.

Both Amy and Andrew are Jewish, and incorporating their heritage into the ceremony was extremely important to them; we built a traditional chuppah in the courtyard of the William Aiken House in downtown Charleston. We edged the chuppah with swathes of silk and velvet and strands of orchids, and ringed it all the way around with chairs. We put a clear-top tent over that, with swags of orange dupioni silk sweeping down from the middle, so that you could see the beauty of the uplit trees in the garden and the starlit sky when it got dark. It was almost like sitting right outside.

Andrew had joked about having attended enough "cookie-cutter" weddings events where, he says, "They might as well have just pointed to a picture, and said 'I'll have wedding package number seven!'" What we wanted to do was to get as far away from that as possible and really make the wedding a direct extension of the couple's personalities. They were both keen on having their friends and family experience Charleston's charm—after all, it was such a large part of Amy's upbringing—but they also wanted a very modern, hip feel to their wedding, rather than one mired in stuffiness and tradition.

SOIRÉE STEP BY STEP:
FLOWER-COVERED CAKE STAND

YOU WILL NEED:

Floral Oasis Designer Block (soaked)
Large Knife
Flowers
Cutting Shears
Plastic Floral Plate or Lomey Dish

Remember to make note of the size of your cake before you try this one; a cake that is very large may not work as well as a smaller cake. Once you determine your size, you'll need some sort of base that won't be seen once you arrange the flowers, but will also contain any water leakage from your oasis. We used a plastic floral base plate to go underneath our cake.

- Place the floral plate on your cake table with the designer block on top, and then set your cake directly on top of the designer block. (Be sure to check with your baker and make sure the cake will not be arriving on a silver platter or other ornamental stand—a round or square flat wooden base will work the best.)

- Once your cake is in place, you can trim the designer block underneath it as necessary to be the same shape and size as your cake.

- Cut your flower stems to about 3 to 4 inches.

- Insert into oasis.

amy and andrew

16 october 2004
charleston, south carolina

SIGNATURE ELEMENTS

QUILT TRIP
Before the wedding, Amy and Andrew asked all their guests to mail them a piece of fabric; once they'd received the final swatch, they had a quilt made. We took that quilt and placed it at the very top of the chuppah, so that even if there were guests who couldn't make it, a little reminder would still be present at the ceremony.

MAKE YOUR MATCH
All our materials played off of one another. In the tent, we hung modern cylindrical lamps, covered with orange dupioni silk and edged with red silk ribbon; we did the same for our standing lamps, which we placed alongside white banquettes covered in orange and red pillows. Even the yarmulkes worn by the men were fall-friendly orangey-red suede!

BEST BUDS
Because orchids are edible, we often like to use them to accessorize food and drink. For this wedding, we placed a tiny yellow and red bloom in each champagne glass, and garnished each slice of wedding cake with the same.

LOCAL FLAVOR
We wanted the burlap guest bags to have an unequivocal Charleston feel but still be light-hearted and fun. We filled them with all manner of lowcountry-themed favors, including benne seed wafers, the latest issue of Charleston magazine, pecans, Charleston Chew candies, and even—as a tribute to the "palmetto bugs" that crawl all over the South—a package of novelty chocolate cockroaches!

BE THERE OR BE SQUARE
When you're doing a seated dinner, it gives a great, streamlined look if you can play up a certain continuity on the table. Because we had square tables, we decided to go with a theme, and do square chargers and square menu cards as well. Each centerpiece was a large square glass vase with a smaller square vase—wrapped in orange dupioni silk—within it.

YOU GOT SERVED
I love presenting food in unexpected, interesting ways. As a surprise for Amy, we served orange sorbet in little red votives as an intermezzo and accompanied each with a tiny espresso spoon. Our caterer, j.b.c. catering, also did oyster stew shooters in espresso cups and miniature crab cakes served on Chinese spoons.

OPPOSITE, LEFT: *Garnished with an orchid, the wedding cake was coconut, Amy's favorite.* OPPOSITE, RIGHT: *Hot Krispy Kreme doughnuts wrapped to go for favors.*

eat and enjoy!
love,
amy and andrew

SOIRÉE SECRETS

SETTING THE STAGE

Don't be afraid to reuse your space. We set the chuppah up on what would later become our dance floor. We made it plain white, rather than black and white—so it was more of a neutral background—and encircled it with chairs. After the ceremony, when people went upstairs for dinner, we moved the chuppah and put a banquette underneath it, so that it became a seating nook. When people came downstairs again, the place where they'd been sitting a few hours earlier during the wedding vows became the place where they dipped, twirled, and boogied into the night.

PASSING TRAYS

I find plain silver trays so boring for passed hors d'oeuvres! Try and liven them up a little bit with something fun and unexpected! One of our hors d'oeuvres was tuna tartare on a wonton crisp. We went with the Asian feel of the wonton and placed each one on a rolled bamboo place mat , which we accessorized with a bright orangey-red dahlia and verdant green banana leaves atop a wooden tray. People love having something pretty to look at—even when the food is phenomenal!

CAKE STAND

A fresh flower-covered cake stand looks beautiful, but it can get pretty costly if you've chosen high-priced blooms. Though we did use red dahlias to complement those in the centerpieces and the bridesmaid's bouquets, we made up the bulk of the cake stand base with orange carnations. When they're all packed together, they can look very beautiful—and they're certainly far less expensive.

FAVORS

There's nothing wrong with mixing high and low culture to add a little bit of frivolous flair. Because Krispy Kreme donuts are unapologetically Southern, we decided to package them for after-dinner favors. While the guests were dancing, one of my staff went to pick up a huge order of the "HOT NOW" sugary treats; we placed them in little boxes tied with red and orange dupioni silk ribbons, and finished them with a card that said "Eat and enjoy!" Needless to say, they were a huge hit!

PRINTS CHARMING

We created miniature printed materials for this wedding, which is one of my absolute favorite things. Our ceremony program was a 3 x 3 square, which folded out into a much more extensive booklet. Correspondingly, the guide we included in the guest bag was also a small square, and featured the same colors and type—a very simple, modern orange font on white card—which folded out. We hand-wrote our butler cards—there were only 120 guests, so we could indulge in little details like that—and our favor boxes were accompanied by an orange tag on which we used the same font as the program and guest tags.

HAPPY ENDINGS

Andrew summed it up best when he said to me, "Nobody else has ever had a wedding like ours, and nobody else will ever have a wedding like ours." What he and Amy liked best about their special day, he said, was that the whole event "had a hip, contemporary feel to it, without being too trendy and in danger of dating itself." The couple went back to New York, where they're still currently living, with a new appreciation of old Southern charm—and I wouldn't be surprised if half their guests are making plans to move down here!

in full bloom

Jenny Hackenberg & Joe Keenan

An outdoor wedding under the oaks at a centuries-

old plantation burst with color as cheery Gerbera

daisies in vivid hues formed the basis of a design

that seamlessly wove the natural world with

natural history.

COUPLING

Joe and Jenny met through friends when they were both living in Raleigh, North Carolina. The proposal, says Jenny, was pretty unexpected; it came on a Monday night! She'd been away on business, and when she got back into town—the two were living in Charleston, where Joe grew up—he took her out for dinner. "I was starving and I ordered all this food, while he said he felt sick and hardly ordered anything," she remembers. "He popped the question right before dinner, and I was so excited, that all of a sudden I was the one who couldn't eat a thing!"

RIGHT: *It was important to Jenny and Joe to be married beneath the huge live oak on the grounds of the plantation—both wanted to feel the history of the place all around them.* OPPOSITE, ABOVE: *Jenny carried a bouquet of white Gerbera daisies, lily of the valley, and white garden roses.* OPPOSITE, BELOW: *Jenny is dressed in a strapless A-line ivory gown by Vera Wang.*

ABOVE, LEFT: *Peach bengaline linens made a feminine addition to round tables, complementing the simple white banquettes bedecked with matching pillows.*

SETTING THE SCENE: DESIGN & DÉCOR

I met with Jenny and Joe for a tasting, and we started discussing ideas for the wedding. Jenny is an interior designer, so she was full of suggestions, but she couldn't decide on a favorite color or theme. All of a sudden, Joe said, "Jenny, you love Gerbera daisies! I gave you some once, remember? They're your favorite flower!" And I said, "Well, there we have it—that's our theme."

Our location was the romantic Drayton Hall Plantation on the outskirts of Charleston. Both Jenny and Joe were adamant about getting married outside, specifically under the huge live oak on the grounds. It tied in with our daisy theme perfectly; we made the decor very organic, in keeping with our natural surroundings. We used the daisies everywhere, in pinks and peaches and oranges and yellows: lining the aisle with them and tying them to the backs of the chairs.

Because we had more than 500 guests, we decided on two tents; the first for the dance floor and the food stations—Jenny and Joe wanted a lowcountry buffet, rather than a sit-down dinner—and the second to contain the bars and our lounge areas. I rented some beautiful antique daybeds, and glued Gerbera daisies to the tops of three-foot tall glass vases, which I filled with candles; it was almost as though they were natural floor lamps. For overhead lighting, we ringed the tops and bottoms of hanging cylindrical lamps with Gerberas. We used peach bengaline linens on the tables and bars and had pillows made to match for the banquets and daybeds.

SOIRÉE STEP BY STEP:
LOWCOUNTRY LEMONADE

YOU WILL NEED:

(per glass)
1 Zombie glass
Crushed Ice
1 ounce Peach Schnapps
Lemonade
Garnish of your choice

We use pink or regular lemonade, depending on the color we want to achieve. You can also change the color to blue by using a small amount of Blue Curaçao or to red by using Grenadine.

- Fill a Zombie glass with plenty of crushed ice.

- Add the Schnapps.

- Fill the remainder with lemonade.

- Use fresh mint to garnish or add a flower, but make sure that it's not a poisonous one!

SIGNATURE ELEMENTS

HIS AND HERS

Jenny had thirteen bridesmaids, and each carried a bouquet of Gerberas in a solid color. For a simple but effective touch, we matched the groomsmen's boutonnieres according to which girl they were going to accompany down the aisle. It wasn't immediately obvious, but when they paired off, it made the procession look very streamlined and put-together.

BRANCHING OUT

Because we had two tents, we had a lot of space to fill. I needed something very high to stand out amongst all those people, so I created several Gerbera daisy "trees." We were given permission to gather sticks from the grounds of the plantation—literally tying in both history and nature to the décor!—which we then planted in deep black urns, accessorizing the limbs with tight clusters of Gerberas of varying colors. The effect was stunning.

HOW DOES YOUR GARDEN GROW?

Because we had so many Gerbera daisies in our décor, we wanted to do something a little different for the centerpieces, so that they weren't just straightforward vases of flowers. We grew rye grass in pots especially for the occasion—it only takes about a week and it's a pretty vibrant green—and then stuck a few Gerberas in with it. It looked so outdoorsy and natural, and it was so much fun to grow it rather than use something fake!

LET'S DANCE

We eschewed the typical black-and-white "checkerboard" pattern for our dance floor, and designed something that more resembled a square dartboard, with alternating black and white lines. The music and dancing were very important to Joe and Jenny—they had three different musical ensembles—and we wanted the dance floor to reflect that.

SPARKLE AND SHINE

At the end, we had each guest take a sparkler, which we'd threaded through a Gerbera daisy, so that essentially, when you were holding your sparkler, you were also holding the couple's signature flower! It was a fun way to add a little bit of a personalized twist to a fairly standard custom.

LEFT: *Simple but effective, plain wooden chairs were made pretty with a swathe of ribbon and a cheery Gerbera daisy affixed to the back.* OPPOSITE, RIGHT: *Gerbera daisy tie-backs provided a splash of whimsy to tent decor.*

SOIRÉE SECRETS

RAIN PLAN

At an outdoor wedding, you always have to be prepared for whatever Mother Nature throws at you. I own two or three hundred white golf umbrellas for occasions like this, so we decorated large pots with Gerbera daisies and placed the umbrellas inside, just in case the heavens decided to open. Luckily, it ended up being dry and sunny—so sunny, in fact, that some of the guests used the umbrellas as parasols for shade!

GIFTS

If you're still looking for that perfect bridesmaid's gift, consider a wrap or pashmina that will go with their dresses. Sure, it'll look pretty and keep them warm. But even better, in an emergency, a pashmina can double as wardrobe saver. On Jenny's big day, one of her bridesmaids left the strapless top to her ensemble back at the house—an hour and a half away from the ceremony location! Luckily, her wrap was almost the same shade of champagne, so we tied it around her in the same fashion. It worked in a pinch, and you can hardly tell in the pictures!

THE GREAT OUTDOORS

Bug spray and candles will only do so much at an outdoor wedding. If you don't want your poor guests to be scratching their arms and ankles every five seconds, invest in a few machines known as Mosquito Magnets, which run off of propane. We found ours at a home improvement store, and we set them out six weeks in advance. Honestly, I'd say they saved our wedding! There's nothing more miserable than being bitten by mosquitoes or gnats while you're trying to concentrate on the vows.

FIREWORKS

While a fireworks display is incredibly dramatic, it can also be incredibly expensive—especially if you hire a professional to set them off for you (and for safety's sake, you really should). For a less costly alternative, consider buying a couple of "cakes" of fireworks; they look like large hatboxes, and once you light the top, they set off a four-minute fireworks display. We set off a few right at the end of the reception, while the guests waved sparklers. It was a lovely surprise for Jenny and Joe.

PRINTS CHARMING

We used a gorgeous French paper in cream for our invitations, and had a calligrapher write them and then hand-paint a single Gerbera daisy onto each. They were pretty dramatic and really beautiful. Our other written materials—ceremony programs and save-the-date cards—followed the same theme: a lone Gerbera daisy in orange.

HAPPY ENDINGS

We surprised Jenny and Joe with a fireworks display as the reception was winding down; they had no idea it was coming! We decorated their getaway car, a vintage Rolls Royce, with—what else?—two bunches of Gerbera daisies wrapped in a white satin ribbon. Jenny told me that her favorite part of the whole planning experience was having someone to help her focus her ideas and make sure everything went as it was supposed to. "If anything major had gone wrong," she says with a laugh, "I never would have known about it."

RIGHT: *Jenny was the first bride to get dressed in the old plantation house at Drayton Hall, a building that made a fitting backdrop for the sense of history both she and Joe wanted to incorporate into the day.*

green day

Lee Boren & Kevin Kleinhelter

An Atlanta couple's shared new last name, the bride's contemporary tastes, and a vivid punch of bright green paired with deep chocolate brown formed the inspiration for this hip, chic wedding infused with low-key sophistication.

COUPLING

When North Carolina native Lee opened her home décor store in Atlanta, she knew it was going to mean a lot of changes in her life; what she didn't know, however, was that one of them would be meeting her future husband. Kevin was the contractor on the project, and as the two spent more and more time together, hashing out the details of the store, a romance grew.

After a year of dating, Kevin popped the question. "He's not a fancy or a formal person, so doing it in a restaurant wouldn't have been very him," says Lee. Instead, Kevin—who had been palling around with Lee's golden retriever, Teddy, for a while—tied a note around the dog's neck that said, "Will you marry me?" And of course, the bride said "yes." Though, she laughs, "Of course, now he's stuck fixing everything in the store!"

RIGHT: *Lee and Kevin make their way through downtown Charleston for the reception at the Yacht Club.* OPPOSITE, ABOVE: *Bridesmaids' bouquets of Brazilia berries and green cymbidium orchids.*

OPPOSITE, BELOW: *Simple yet striking, Lee's bouquet comprised gardenias, snowberries, and white orchids with a green throat.*

SETTING THE SCENE: DESIGN & DÉCOR

Lee was a lot of fun to work with, because we love all the same things; her taste is modern, but also still fairly classic. In fact, we discovered that several pictures she'd torn out of magazines for inspiration had turned out to be Soirée weddings—she just hadn't known it! We went with the combination of bright pea green and chocolate brown because she'd used a similar color palette for her store.

The two were married at the French Huguenot Church in downtown Charleston, with the reception at a local private club. Because the room was enormous, we decorated it in such a way as to cut off all the corners, thereby shrinking it. We built several 8 x 8-foot cabanas to break up the room, which we tented with a bright green fabric. Guests loved having these private little rooms alongside the dance floor, in which they could sit and catch up with relatives they hadn't seen in a while. We added a sheer sweeping panel of organza and placed a white sofa in each.

For the main space, we built banquettes and covered them with white fabric and topped them with green pillows edged in white; alongside and in front of them, we placed ottomans covered in chocolate brown bengaline fabric, with white piping and inverted pleats. We used large, round paper lanterns throughout the room, which added to the clean, modern feel.

SOIRÉE STEP BY STEP:
CUSTOM FLOWER MONOGRAM

YOU WILL NEED:

1 large piece of foam board from your local art store, 1/4 inch thick
Scissors
Pencil
Mums
Hot glue gun and plenty of glue sticks
Floral wire or zip ties
Floral cutting shears

- Trace or sketch your letter onto the foam core.

- Cut out the letter.

- Cut the stems completely off of your mums so that you are left with only flower heads.

- Using the floral wire or a zip tie, wrap it around a few places of your letter to create a hanging mechanism or hook just like a picture frame. It's better to do this before you apply the flowers so that you don't harm the finished product later.

- With a hot glue gun, apply the heads to the foam core, covering it completely. This can be done, at the most, one day prior to your event. Mums are pretty sturdy flowers and should last a day without water.

SIGNATURE ELEMENTS

GRASS ROOTS

Because rye grass is exactly the vivid green we were using in our color palette, we grew trays of it and then placed each one in a box that we'd covered with white and chocolate-colored ribbon. We added a tall glass vase, which we filled with a candle, placed the whole thing on top of cubes of chocolate brown fabric, and put them in front of the sofa in each cabana. They were part table, part window box, and they looked stunning.

PIECE OF CAKE

Lee didn't want a traditional wedding cake, so we decided to get pretty funky with the idea instead, drawing on her interior design background. We did five different flavored cakes in varying designs—polka dots, stripes, flowers—and each one was decorated with some combination of green, brown, and white. Displayed on a long cake table together, they looked fantastic: so hip and contemporary.

INITIAL THOUGHTS

Taking a new last name is a big step, and we wanted to play on that by highlighting the K for Kleinhelter, since it would be something the couple would share forever. We had square stickers printed, which we affixed to our guest bags; they, in turn, contained a bottle of water, green tea soap—even our flavors went with our green theme!—and a box of green M&Ms, all marked with a K.

SMALL WORLD

Instead of a sit-down dinner, we had heavy hors d'oeuvres at separate food stations. To make it fun, we did all our food in miniature portions—baby crab cakes, baby fried green tomatoes, and tiny servings of shrimp and grits in scallop shells. We also had little cones of sweet potato fries and mini grilled cheese sandwiches with tomato basil soup, served in espresso cups.

PEAS, PLEASE

I love using something from the natural world that's exactly the hue of our color palette. For this wedding, I thought that bright green dried peas would be perfect. The chef used them to line some of the trays we used to serve food. We also poured them into tall shot glasses and used them as holders for the pens at the sign-in station.

OPPOSITE, RIGHT: *Inspired by the décor, some guests even arrived in green and brown ensembles!*

SOIRÉE SECRETS

ROOM TRANSFORMATION

The room we were working with was not only cavernous, but didn't have enough of a personality to hold up on its own; it almost felt like a school gym. To get around a problem like this, we like to cover the whole room with fabric, swathing it from the center of the ceiling out to the walls. It creates a gorgeous, dreamy effect; plus it lowers your ceiling a little to make the room a little more intimate and a little less like an auditorium. It's a great way to transform a room that's not working for you.

CREATING A LOUNGE

I love taking two sofas and arranging them back to back, then putting a sofa table in between them. You don't even need a real sofa table; we just take a conference table and then add PVC piping onto the legs to make it taller! These tables are real multi-taskers: they give you a place to put easy décor pieces like candles and flowers and—if the flowers are tall enough—provide a bit of privacy between sofas. Best of all, guests have a place to reach back and put their cocktails, which means you don't have to add extra side tables or ottomans in front of them.

THEMED DECOR

If you're going to be using an initial in a lot of your décor, like we did with our K, make sure you're re-creating exactly the same character, no matter the size. To ensure that our large foam board K covered in green mums—which we hung from the railing outside the church—was the exact same K we were using on our printed materials and in our guest bags, we took one letter and photocopied it in a variety of sizes. When we came to make the large foam board, we took the blown-up K and traced around it, to ensure it matched the others perfectly.

PRETTY PACKAGES

Your attendants are an important part of your ceremony. It's a nice touch to present their bouquets and boutonnieres to them in an appealing, attractive way. We lined the boxes for our boutonnieres and bouquets with wax tissue paper in the signature bright green. Then we packaged them in white bags with green tissue paper, and hung each person's name card from them with brown ribbon. If you can deliver each attendant's flowers in a pretty package like that, it's sure to be appreciated.

PRINTS CHARMING

Lee uses a lot of squares in her designs for the store, and so all of our printed materials were square too—the invitations, the save-the-date cards, the programs—and they all had a second square, containing the "K" for Kleinhelter, inside them. We went with a very simple brown and white design, and tied the programs and the guest bags with a bright green ribbon. For our sign-in station, we had guests write their wishes for Lee and Kevin on square note cards with the "K" at the top. It's lovely when everything matches, especially when it's such a simple, clean concept.

HAPPY ENDINGS

As guests waved sparklers they'd lit with lighters bearing a "K" on them, Lee and Kevin left the reception in a vintage Rolls Royce. On the back, instead of a "Just Married" sign, we'd attached the "K" made from mums, that had been on the railing of the French Huguenot Church.

RIGHT: *Flower girl Madison Kleinhelter carried a miniature version of the bridesmaids' bouquets: Brazilia berries and green cymbidium orchids.*

small wonder

Martha Patrick & Jon Robbins

An all-white ceremony, an intimate dinner at a small

local restaurant, and an impeccable attention to detail

made this understated wedding for forty a study in

modest, unassuming charm.

Welcome to Charleston!

COUPLING

Martha and Jon met through Soirée; it turns out we're not just an event planning firm but a matchmaking one as well! Martha runs the Lettered Olive, Soirée's graphic design division, and Jon's brother is our rental company's manager. He had just moved to Charleston from Los Angeles, so he and Martha were introduced through work.

After three years of dating, talk turned to marriage. Martha's family owns a jewelry store in her hometown of Columbus, Georgia, "so Jon knew he'd have to get the ring there!" she laughs. They picked it out together over Christmas, and then spent the afternoon running errands, before Jon officially asked Martha to marry him. "It was funny, because while I knew he had the ring in his pocket," she recalls, "I just didn't know exactly when it was coming!"

RIGHT: *Blooming pear branches and vases of fully-opened French white tulips made for a truly heavenly display at the altar.*
OPPOSITE BELOW: *Out-of-town guests were greeted with cheery welcome boxes containing lowcountry delights like benne seed wafers, Charleston Chews, pralines, and an informative miniature guest booklet, whose grommets matched those on the ceremony program.*

ABOVE: *Tiny French bistro La Fourchette, in Charleston's trendy Upper King neighborhood, closed its doors on Saturday evening to host and honor Martha and Jon.*

SETTING THE SCENE: DESIGN & DÉCOR

Martha and I have worked together on so many weddings that I was thrilled to have her as a client and to finally be able to create something beautiful and meaningful just for her. She wanted a very small affair, just forty or so guests, and she was adamant that no one would have to work too hard either before or during the wedding. Because she'd been on the other side of all the effort and planning on so many occasions, she wanted everyone to just enjoy the day. She eschewed grand details like a tent and a band in favor of an intimate dinner party reception at local French restaurant, La Fourchette.

We kept the ceremony décor very simple. Everything was white—very clean and classic. Martha looked like a beautiful, demure Audrey Hepburn in her dress (which I helped her pick out) with a full skirt and simple lines; we made sure the feel of her wedding matched that very sweet, unpretentious, unfussy look. She loves tulips, so we made abundant use of them, and our signature color for the reception was red, "Which just sort of happened," says Martha, "because I knew I didn't want pink."

SOIRÉE STEP BY STEP:

CENTERPIECE WITH LEAF AND ANEMONE

YOU WILL NEED:

Glass cylinder vases
Anemones
Flowers for filling vases (we used tulips)
Flower cutting shears
Glue gun with glue sticks
Aspidistra leaves

- Wrap your leaf around the glass vase and secure it in place with the hot glue.

- Using the cutting shears, cut one of your anemone stems off so that you are left with only the head.

- Hot glue the flower head onto the leaf, covering up the same spot where you earlier glued.

- Fill your vases with the remaining flowers.

SIGNATURE ELEMENTS

BLOOM WITH A VIEW

The flowers in the French Huguenot Church were some of the favorites that I've done. I filled huge urns with blooming pear branches for the altar, and in front of them I filled glass cylinders with bunches and bunches of white tulips. They almost looked like a magnolia bloom, they opened so wide. In front of the vases, I lined two rows of tiny clear votive cups and placed white candles in them. The arrangement was so beautiful—though, of course, it didn't take away from our bride!

MARCH OF THE PENGUINS

Martha told me she was a big fan of edible favors—in fact, I think her exact words were, "If I can't eat it or drink it, I don't want it!" So we ordered chocolate truffles from Burdick Chocolates in the shape of tiny penguins—Jon's father loves penguins—and wrapped the boxes in red ribbons. They were cute and stylish, and all the guests loved how original they were.

IT'S A SMALL WORLD

Instead of a traditional wedding cake, Martha wanted something a little more understated. Besides, with the reception taking place in such a small restaurant, she says, "there wasn't really anywhere to put a big cake!" So, together with baker Jim Smeal, we came up with the idea of individual, miniature cakes—one for each guest. They were chocolate and kahlua with vanilla buttercream, just one layer high, and we even managed to re-create the red dandelion from the invitations on top of each one.

LITTLE SURPRISE

Okay, what woman doesn't love handbags! A fabulous local designer and personal friend, Allison Abney, surprised Martha the morning of her wedding with a custom silk clutch in bright red, the day's signature hue. It was the perfect accessory for the perfect day.

LEFT: *Martha wanted an all-white bouquet, which we made from tulips, gardenias, and ranunculuses.* OPPOSITE, LEFT: *Personalized invitations in letter form brought a hint of the cozy, less informal affair to come.* OPPOSITE, RIGHT: *Miniature programs made a pretty splash.*

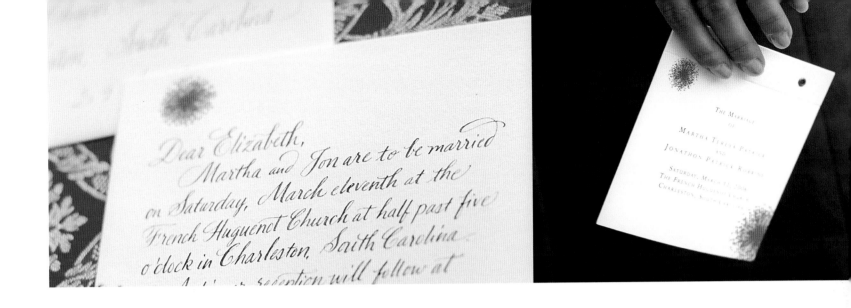

SOIRÉE SECRETS

CASUAL CORRESPONDENCE

For a less formal feel, consider forgoing the traditional wording on your invitation and, instead, send out something that more resembles a letter. Because Martha had a very small wedding, we hand-wrote each of her invitations, addressing guests by their first names, and signing each one from her parents. It was the first indication to guests of what an intimate, individualized affair it was going to be.

PRINTING TEMPLATES

Martha liked the design of her dandelion-adorned invitations so much that she had a bunch of extras printed up and then had the calligrapher write on them afterwards. She used them for table numbers, favor signage, and even thank-you notes after the wedding. It's a great way to tie your design together.

PLACE CARDS

A great way to add a little custom flair while simultaneously saving a bit of money is to double up on your menu cards and place cards. Martha had the calligrapher add the name of each guest to the top of her menu cards in a larger script so guests knew where to sit. That way, the menus pulled double duty and guests had personalized keepsakes to take home with them.

ALTERNATIVE ATTIRE

Don't be afraid to think outside the strapless Vera Wang when it comes to your wedding dress. With only three months between the engagement and the wedding, Martha didn't really have enough time to have a gown fitted and made, so I helped her pick out a white silk bridesmaid's dress by designer Siri. Since she wanted a short dress anyway, she said, it worked perfectly. Even better? Bridesmaid gowns are a lot less costly!

PRINTS CHARMING

Because Martha is incredibly creative, she wanted to design all of her own printed materials. The recurring red dandelion motif was a piece of art taken from a book she owned, and it ended up looking so beautiful in print that we decided to take the red and run with it. As well as her invitations, which were written in calligraphy, she also designed the stickers for her gift boxes, her miniature ceremony programs—to which she added grommets; Martha loves the look of grommets!—and her menu cards.

HAPPY ENDINGS

"I didn't want a big fuss to be made," says Martha of her big day. "I didn't want to fight a hundred people to go to the bathroom, and I wanted everyone to be able to talk and make toasts and be heard properly." As such, it seems we certainly delivered; several guests commented on the personalized, intimate feel of the occasion. And when it was time to leave the reception, "We didn't leave in a car; we just walked out and went to a bar, then walked to a hotel," laughs Martha. "It was pretty simple and low-key."

dinner at tiffany's

Claire Strang & Jake Farver

Wrapped up with ribbons and bedecked with full white buds at every turn, this graceful Tiffany blue–themed wedding gave Holly Golightly a run for her money in terms of clean, crisp elegance, and delicate signature touches.

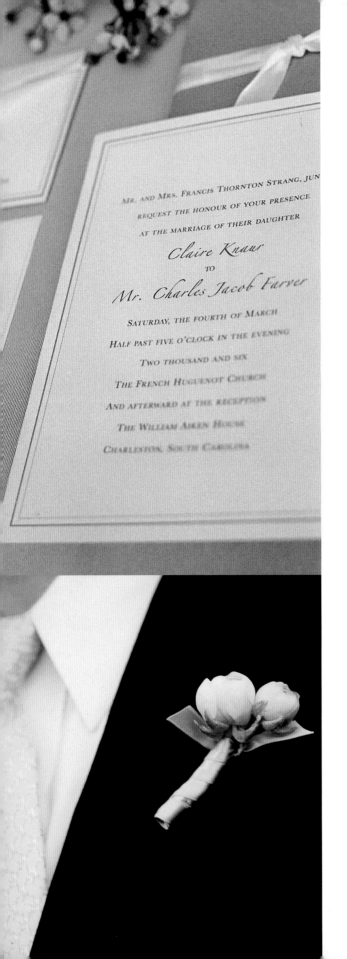

COUPLING

Claire and Jake met in college during her junior year—purely by accident. When Claire's date to a social function canceled on her, mutual friends suggested that Jake might be a good stand-in. Claire agreed to this blind date and, much to her surprise, found herself falling for the handsome sophomore.

After graduation, Claire, a native of Chattanooga, Tennessee, moved from North Carolina to Washington, D.C., and a year later Jake followed. One sunny Sunday morning in April, six years after they'd first started dating, Jake suggested they take his boat out, as the weather hadn't been good enough to allow them to do so yet. "I did wonder why he was up at the crack of dawn," laughs Claire, "but apparently he was just so nervous." The two moored the boat in a small cove, and Jake turned to Claire and asked her to be his wife. "I was shocked!" she recalls. "I think I said, 'If I'd known you were going to ask, I would at least have put on some makeup!'"

RIGHT: *Tables outside on the porch of the William Aiken House were swathed in Tiffany blue bengaline fabric and lit with votives. Simple white cane chairs with white cushions completed the effect.* OPPOSITE, ABOVE: *Pretty letterpress invitations tied with a white ribbon set the scene for the wedding's unparalleled grace.* OPPOSITE, BELOW: *Each groomsmen's boutonniere was a ranunculus bud tied with Tiffany blue ribbon.*

ABOVE, RIGHT: *Gift boxes filled with monogrammed soap were wrapped in Tiffany blue ribbon and presented with a card bearing each guest's name.* OPPOSITE: *Custom-made shadow box coffee tables filled with votives containing gardenias gave guests something pretty to look at in the lounge tent.*

SETTING THE SCENE: DESIGN & DÉCOR

In the early stages of planning her wedding, Claire and I were still trying to come up with a theme and a color palette; we'd talked about it a little, but nothing had jumped out at either of us. Then one day she came by our offices in a really pretty Tiffany blue skirt. I complimented her on the shade, and, before I knew it, we'd decided to make it our signature color for the wedding. I just love when something jumps out at you on the spot; often, the idea is right in front of you.

We decided to pair the Tiffany blue with white; it's such a strong, distinctive shade that it needs a simple color as its complement. After the ceremony at the French Huguenot Church, guests went to the William Aiken House where we'd put up a clear-top tent in the garden alongside the dining room and furnished it with banquette seating. This wedding had such a distinct and elegant feel, we felt chandeliers, rather than lanterns, would be more fitting.

The linens we used for the tables—a simple bengaline in Tiffany blue—were the same fabric as the bridesmaid's dresses! And because we were already using a color so inextricably linked with the world's most famous jewelry store, we thought it would be a cute idea to take it one step further and play off the idea of the jewelry box. As such, we used a lot of ribbon for a very "finished" feel: on the invitations, in the wreath outside the church, and, of course, wrapped around the gift boxes and favor boxes. The overall result was very graceful and refined—perfect for an elegant Southern girl.

SOIRÉE STEP BY STEP:
SHADOW BOX TABLE

Top:
1 x 4-foot piece of wood
1/2-inch-thick piece of plywood

Bottom:
3/4-inch-thick piece of plywood
Paint and paintbrush
Screws
Drill
Glass, cut to size*
Votives
Flowers
Fabric
Fabric scissors
Staple gun

* Make sure you have your glass cut at a professional glass shop to ensure that it's the correct thickness and the edges are polished.

- Determine the size of your table. This table consists of a few pieces: the ottoman style box for support on the bottom and the open shadow box on the top.

- Build a box similar to the one on page 157 for the Ice Table, using the 1 x 4-foot wood for the sides and a plywood piece for the bottom.

- Build another ottoman-style box using the larger sheets of the 3/4-inch plywood. Cut a square for the top and the same size squares for the sides. Screw the sides together at right angles, creating a box, and secure the top with screws as well. Do not create a bottom; keep one end open.

- Cover your bottom base box with fabric using a staple gun, and attaching the fabric to the top and insides. Set the top box on top of your base box.

- Fill the inside of your top box with votives spread out proportionately to fill it entirely. Fill each votive with a small amount of water and a cut flower in each one.

- Place a piece of cut glass on top to create the table.

SIGNATURE ELEMENTS

OUTSIDE THE BOX

I love taking plain, simple pieces and giving them a quick makeover to match the colors of the wedding. While we could have used clear glass vases for our centerpieces, I wanted to incorporate as much of the Tiffany blue as I could, so we painted small wooden boxes the exact shade of our table linens, then filled them with blooming pear branches, roses, and ranunculuses to complement Claire's bouquet. They looked so pretty—and they smelled heavenly!

TRUE BLUE

We dressed up our Lowcountry Lemonade for the occasion, adding a drop of blue curaçao to the peach Schnapps and lemonade and lining the rims with sugar. Instead of adding a flower to each, we tied a tiny piece of Tiffany blue ribbon to a clear plastic swizzle stick and placed it into each glass, in a subtle nod to the same ribbons we'd used in the wreath in front of the church.

TO THE LETTER

For Claire's favors, which were gardenia-scented soaps, we were originally going to monogram each with an "F" for Farver, their shared new last name. The mother of the bride, however, came up with an excellent idea: why not tailor the initial to the last name of each guest instead? So we did! Our calligrapher created individual labels bearing each guest's name, then we placed the soaps in white boxes and tied them with a Tiffany blue ribbon. They looked just like the coveted jewelry boxes, though with the colors reversed.

SHOW YOUR STRIPES

Because Claire's dress was ridged with subtle stripes, we thought it would be a particularly chic touch to replicate them on her cake as well. She wanted a very simple cake, so we made sure the detail was very delicate and understated. Each of the five tiers was striped to match her dress, and then we edged the bottom in a Tiffany blue ribbon. The effect was gorgeous: very simple but effective.

SWEET FIZZ

Although a champagne toast with the cutting of the cake is lovely in itself, we wanted to dress it up a little in keeping with our theme. We took tiny scoops of lemon sorbet, which was colored blue, and placed each one in a champagne flute. I love sorbet with champagne; I think it's so elegant. And what a novel way to add a little more blue!

LEFT: *The entrance to the William Aiken House was softened with billowing drapes and a hanging chandelier.* OPPOSITE, LEFT: *"Wedding wands" tied with white streamers of ribbon made an original alternative to fireworks for the big send-off.* OPPOSITE, RIGHT: *Outside the French Huguenot Church, the wreath of dahlias and roses was adorned with tiny blue "love knots" tied in a narrow ribbon.*

SOIRÉE SECRETS

ROSE WREATH

If you're working with a color like Tiffany blue, you're probably going to be hard-pressed to find flowers in exactly the right shade. Rather than settle for something less than perfect in our wreath, we used easy-to-find white flowers, but worked in our signature hue with ribbon instead. We tied tiny "love knots" in each piece, then scattered them amongst our white roses and dahlias. Voila: we had an elegant wreath with a subtle splash of signature color, without having to resort to a less-than-perfect shade.

WEDDING WANDS

Sparklers make for a dazzling send-off, for sure, but if you want a slightly safer option—perhaps you're expecting a lot of children at your wedding, or have been asked by the reception site not to violate fire safety policy—there is an equally striking alternative. We call them "wedding wands," and we got the idea from an old movie; they're wooden dowels wrapped with long streamers of ribbon at the end. We placed them in white buckets—the display looked fabulous —and had each guest take one to wave as the bride and groom departed. It looked magical—all those ribbons flying at once—and there was no fear that we'd burn the building down!

CAKE PLACEMENT

Although it's fairly standard practice to place your wedding cake on a table in the middle of the room, you might consider a relocation if your reception site comes with exquisite pieces of furniture ready to be used. The sideboard on which we displayed Claire's cake was just begging to be used in some way. The painting hanging in the background and the sconces on either side framed the cake beautifully, and there was enough room for us to place large vases of white tulips on either side. It was artsy and discreet and blended in with the sophistication of the room, rather than demanding attention from the middle.

MAKING AN ENTRANCE

It's incredibly easy to warm up the entrance to your reception. To soften the wrought-iron gates of the William Aiken House, we covered a curtain rod in Tiffany-blue ribbon, placed it between the gates, and draped sheer white fabric from each side to make beautiful, billowing drapes. Because we had chandeliers inside the tent, we thought it would be a nice touch to welcome guests with one outside as well, so we hung it from the very top of the gate. You can always liven up an entrance with lighting and fabric.

PRINTS CHARMING

All of our printed materials were Tiffany blue and white. Our save-the-date cards and guest booklets came in a little Tiffany blue envelope tied with a white ribbon, which foreshadowed the Tiffany jewelry box idea. Our programs and invitations matched as well, as did the stickers on the gift boxes and the labels on the bottled water inside. We used the same font throughout for uniformity, and even replicated the signature line of dots on the white paper napkins, which were printed with the couple's name and wedding date for posterity.

HAPPY ENDINGS

The couple left the reception in a 1981 pearl white Rolls Royce that was called, appropriately enough, the "Audrey Hepburn." Of her wedding, Claire says, "It was so beautiful and so different. I'd been in ten weddings, so I felt like I'd seen everything there was to see. I wanted something unique, and that's exactly what I got. It was just like a vacation—everyone had so much fun."

RIGHT: *Tall Tiffany-inspired boxes welcomed out-of-town guests to Charleston with personalized bottled water, a helpful visitor's booklet, and colorful thumbprint cookies, shipped from Claire's hometown of Chattanooga, Tennessee.*

Welcome to Charleston!

Love,

Claire and Jake

Chattanooga Thumbprint Cookies

Claire and Jake

Dear Family and Fri

Welcome to Charleston! We are to
have ya'll here for our wedding wee
This is such a special time for us, mad
better because yo—

Welcome to Charleston

We hope this boo
give you the information t
enjoy your stay to work as the

grecian grace

Margaret Anne Florence & Peter Siachos

Weaving their treasured Greek heritage into every aspect of this culture-rich wedding, an urban New York couple with strong Southern roots proves that you can come home again—and you can do it with style.

COUPLING

Oddly enough, Margaret Anne and Peter first met at her cousin's wedding when their families were seated at the same table; though they chatted, she had a boyfriend at the time, and nothing came of their meeting. Then, five years later, Margaret Anne happened to see Peter at a restaurant in her native Charleston. While she didn't remember where she'd met him before until some time later, the friend she'd been with happened to know Peter and gave Margaret Anne his e-mail address. She got in touch, they laughed over the coincidence, and the romance blossomed from there.

When Peter proposed on Valentine's Day, Margaret Anne, an actress and singer, was working part-time in a headshot studio in New York. Unbeknownst to her, Peter had arranged with her photographer boss to let him come in that day and surprise her by getting down on one knee to ask for her hand. He even arranged it so that her boss was poised to capture the whole thing on film, making for one truly spectacular Kodak moment.

RIGHT: *With scrollwork taken from Margaret Anne's dress and a color palette drawn from the ensembles of the bridesmaids, the cake was a work of art and drew oohs and aahs from impressed guests.*
OPPOSITE, ABOVE: *Though her career as an actress and singer meant she was used to having all eyes on her, Margaret Anne made a beautiful, demure bride.*

ABOVE, LEFT: *Underneath a commanding arrangement of orchids and lilies in the foyer of the Country Club of Charleston, boxes of rose petals and sugared almonds awaited guests.* OPPOSITE: *Handmade with love by Peter's family, a cornucopia of traditional Greek sweets and confections made for an astounding dessert bar.*

SETTING THE SCENE: DESIGN & DÉCOR

Margaret Anne came to me after having seen my work at several of her friends' weddings. With a reputation to uphold, I got to work immediately on the planning!

Her mother is Greek, as are both of Peter's parents, so right from the beginning we knew that their shared cultural heritage would play a large role in the wedding—from the food to the music to the location, which was the Greek Orthodox Church in downtown Charleston. Margaret Anne told me that her favorite color was purple, and when I saw the bridesmaids' dresses she'd picked out—a pale lavender with a bronze ribbon at the top—we decided to base the whole wedding on those same hues.

When she came to me with a picture from Donald Trump's wedding, with pew markers fashioned from long strings of flowers, I suggested that we do something similar—though far less costly—with vivid purple orchids, which complemented those she carried in her bouquet. For the reception at the Country Club of Charleston, we had a Greek buffet with dishes like spanakopita, moussaka, roast lamb, and Greek salad. We even included several recipes in the welcome boxes for out-of-town guests, which proved very popular with both the Greeks and non-Greeks alike!

SOIRÉE STEP BY STEP:
HAT BOX DESSERT STATION

YOU WILL NEED:

Wooden hat boxes of varying sizes
Latex paint
Paintbrush

- Paint your hat boxes entirely with latex paint in the colors of your choice.

- Arrange the hat boxes in varying heights using both the tops and bottoms for your station.

- You can also use the tops of the hat boxes as serving trays and the bottom as a unique cake stand. If you are using your boxes for food display or serving trays, be sure to cover them with something like parchment paper or leaves to ensure that they're food-safe.

SIGNATURE ELEMENTS

THE SWEETEST THING

Margaret Anne told me she wanted a dessert bar, so rather than display all the traditional Greek sweets on ordinary plates and trays, we found several hat boxes and painted them the same bronze as the ribbons on the bridesmaids' dresses. They looked gorgeous and provided varying heights for our sugary delicacies like baklava, finikia, and kourambiathes (Greek wedding cookies), all of which were made by Peter's family and, impressively, arrived intact after the four-hour car journey from Greenville, South Carolina!

PIECE OF CAKE

Margaret Anne's cake was a masterpiece; it combined elements of both her dress and the dresses of her bridesmaids. From the former, we took the embroidery at the bust and on the train and reproduced it in buttercream on each tier. From the latter, we used the alternating bands of lavender and brown, mimicking the piece of bronze ribbon at the top of the ensemble.

OPA! OPA!

It was so much fun to make an ouzo bar for this wedding. Margaret Anne and Peter weren't quite sure about it at first, because they were a little worried, as Margaret Anne says, "that it might turn into a frat party!" We decided to go ahead with it anyway, and thank goodness, because it proved to be the hit of the night! To give it a little bit more of an upscale feel, I froze the bottles of ouzo in blocks of ice with orchids pressed into them, then nestled them in a bed of crushed ice with frozen shot glasses alongside them.

PLAYING FAVORITES

We packaged boxes of rose petals for guests to take at the end of the reception and throw at Margaret Anne and Peter as they left for their new life. There was a lovely synchronicity to the gesture, as our aisle had been lined with rose petals too. In the same boxes, which we stacked alongside the rose petals, we placed lavender-colored sugared almonds for guests to take as favors.

LEFT: *Pew markers fashioned from strings of purple orchids and topped with a Casablanca lily were tied with bronze ribbon to match the bridesmaids' dresses.*
OPPOSITE: *At the end of the night, a 1962 Ford Starliner made the perfect getaway vehicle for Margaret Anne and Peter, a classic car fanatic.*

SOIRÉE SECRETS

TRADITIONS

If you're holding a wedding with a cultural twist, make sure to keep your guests apprised of the reason behind each tradition. Sugared almonds, for example, are given out at Greek weddings because they're said to symbolize both the sweetness and the bitterness of life. They're traditionally packaged in an uneven number—either five or seven—so that they're not easily divisible, which mirrors the unity of the couple. Because I had no idea about this, and many of the guests didn't either, we printed out an explanation, made it into a sticker, and placed it atop each box of almonds. Similarly, when we passed champagne with pomegranate juice among the guests, we included a tag on it to explain that pomegranate is the Greek symbol of fertility.

FAMILY PHOTOS

Family is so important on a wedding day. If you're going to be entertaining a lot of out-of-town relatives, a great way to make them feel a little more at home—and to give your reception venue more of a cozy, familiar feel—is to set up a personalized gallery. We took framed photographs of both sides of the couple's family, from their parents to their great-grandparents, typed out their names and the date of their wedding, and displayed them on the piano for guests to peruse. We even included a few pictures of Margaret Anne and Peter when they were younger, to make it even more poignant.

FLOWER POWER

An incredibly easy way to save money while maintaining a feeling of continuity is to re-use the flowers you had at the church somewhere in your reception. We took the long strands of orchids that had served as pew markers and tied them to the couple's getaway car; there was more than enough time to transfer them from one place to another. After all, you might as well get as much use from them as you can, because you'll be off on your honeymoon the next day and won't be able to keep them.

PRINTS CHARMING

In designing Margaret Anne's wedding materials, The Lettered Olive recommended that she think outside the box! You don't have to order typical stationery store invitations if that doesn't fit your wedding style. We specialize in creating custom invitation suites that tie your whole event together. From your design, you can create wonderful details by using the same symbol, color, or fonts. It makes for continuity and offers individuality to every aspect of your wedding. From guest booklets and favor packaging, to wedding programs and even your "just married" sign, it's all in the details!

HAPPY ENDINGS

Peter is a classic car–nut, so it was very important to the couple that they leave in something swinging and stylish. In the end, one of Peter's father's friends loaned the couple a '62 Ford Starliner for their getaway car. It was a bright aqua blue, and we decorated it with purple orchids and a printed "Just Married" sign in a font that matched their invitations.

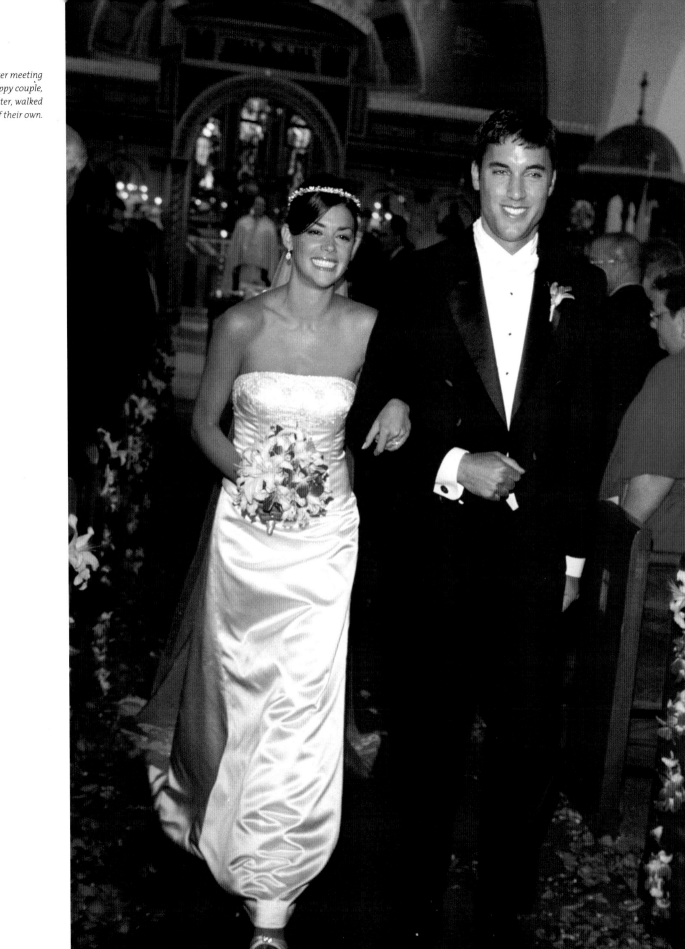

RIGHT: *Eight years after meeting at a wedding, the happy couple, Margaret Anne and Peter, walked down an aisle of their own.*

a hallowed eve

Kate Sobrero & Chris Markgraf

When a professional soccer player and her fiancé chose

Halloween night for their wedding, they were keen to

maximize the holiday's charms without venturing into

the cutesy and twee.

COUPLING

Kate moved from New York to Boston some years ago, and when she arrived, an old friend from school offered to set her up with one of his co-workers—who was, of course, Chris. "But apparently he looked me up on the Internet, and said 'No thanks; I'm not interested!' " laughs the talented member of the U.S. women's soccer team. Still, the friend was persistent about the two meeting, and finally, seven months later, they did. "At first, there really wasn't any spark," recalls Kate. "But over the next two or three weeks, while I was traveling out of town, we emailed back and forth. When I got back to Boston, I was definitely excited about seeing him again. And that time, it just clicked."

A year and a half later, Chris printed out all of those old emails—together with ticket stubs and other mementoes from their courtship—and fashioned them into a book which he presented to Kate. On the last page, he tied a ring to the paper with ribbon and glued a box over the top, next to a picture he'd taken of himself. After urging her to open the box, the crafty Chris asked Kate to marry him. And while she could have mirrored his "No thanks; I'm not interested!" from so long ago, she did, of course, say "yes."

RIGHT: *After a cocktail hour in the rotunda, Kate prepared to make her grand entrance into the dining room of Hibernian Hall.* OPPOSITE, ABOVE: *The groom's boutonniere was fashioned from lily of the valley, stephanotis, and a calla lily.* OPPOSITE, BELOW: *Bridesmaids carried simple bouquets of black calla lilies with lily of the valley leaves.*

ABOVE, LEFT: *Vases of deep red roses made a striking contrast with the crisp white linens.* ABOVE, RIGHT: *So guests could sit and catch up, long white banquettes studded with dark red pillows made for an inviting lounge area against the tall imposing white pillars of Hibernian Hall.*

SETTING THE SCENE: DESIGN & DÉCOR

When I met with the couple, they already knew they wanted to hold the ceremony on Halloween. Kate's college friends have a tradition of getting married on a Friday and spending the weekend together, and the Friday that worked best just happened to be the 31st of October.

We agreed that while we wanted to play off the holiday and incorporate some of the playful elements associated with it, what we didn't want was for the evening to turn into a Halloween party, rather than a wedding. In fact, Kate's exact direction to me was "I want to honor the holiday, but not make it the focal point." Though we used pumpkins in our décor, and incorporated things like the tradition of trick-or-treating, we were careful not to venture into the cheesy.

Kate loved deep, rich, regal reds, so we made them a large part of the night. Because she's a self-confessed tomboy and "not really a big flower person," we eschewed frilliness and fussiness, and decided instead upon a mixture of very deep purple calla lilies for the cake and bouquet, and simple dark red roses for the table centerpieces. The wedding was held at the Second Presbyterian Church in Charleston, and then guests traveled afterwards by private trolley to Hibernian Hall for dinner.

SOIRÉE STEP BY STEP:
HOW TO DRESS YOUR BUTLER CARD TABLE

A seated dinner always requires a butler card table. Instead of doing the same old table with folded tent cards, try something different. Use fruits or vegetables to bring in color and texture. Also depending on your location, you can make any space more interesting with light. For this Halloween wedding, we used pumpkins for the base of the butler cards and placed the table in the center of the room, which happened to be a beautiful rotunda. By hanging velvet fabric from four places at the top of the rotunda, we were able to float a wrought iron lantern filled with candles over the butler cards. It not only defined the space and created a dramatic entrance, but it also provided light for each guest to find their name and table number.

KIE LANGEL
E 10

SIGNATURE ELEMENTS

HELLO, PUMPKIN!

In keeping with the season, we displayed our butler cards on miniature pumpkins, which we lit with a lantern overhead filled with candles and hung from a deep velvet rope. When guests walked into Hibernian Hall, they looked for their name on the pumpkin to know at which table they were sitting. We even had a big jar of candy pumpkins in the middle to set the light-hearted tone of the evening.

SWEETS FOR THE SWEET

For our favors, we thought it would be fun to remind folks that all the neighborhood kids were out trick-or-treating that night, so we changed out the miniature pumpkins we'd had on the table and replaced them with jars of candy—in reds and blacks and oranges, of course. We put mini bags out, so guests could come down and help themselves to sweets to take home with them, just like they'd been trick-or-treating themselves!

FOOD, GLORIOUS FOOD

It was a pretty subtle nod to the date, but we even served pumpkin risotto in hollowed-out miniature pumpkins. Of course, the food was fantastic, but guests loved the presentation too.

CUTTING EDGE

We wanted to line the stage with something other than vases of flowers or glass cylinders holding candles, so our chef carved about twenty pumpkins, and we used those instead. Rather than scary faces, we had pretty shapes and interesting designs, so that we added a floral element without actually using flowers.

LEFT: *Red velvet linens set the scene for the sit-down supper, while candles of varying heights made a nice complement to the flowers at different intervals.* OPPOSITE: *The dining room of Hibernian Hall was alive with chatter as guests tucked into their feast. Classic chandeliers made for an upscale, romantic feel.*

SOIRÉE SECRETS

CENTERPIECES

Don't be afraid to experiment with different heights when it comes to table centerpieces. Because we were really only working with one color with our flowers—that deep, dark red—I wanted to break up the uniformity and add a little interest to the table. We filled silver julep cups with the same black calla lilies we used in Kate's bouquet and around her cake, and then created height by using candlesticks to hold displays of Black Magic roses and Charlotte roses. Candlesticks can make great makeshift vases.

CREATIVE TABLES

Because our main table was very small—just the bride and groom and their respective parents—we didn't want to use the same rectangular tables we'd used for all the other guests. To add a little visual interest, experiment with unusual table shapes. We found that a triangle worked perfectly for six people at this wedding; a couple could sit at each side, and everyone had a perfect view of the room.

AFTER PARTY

Remember that your wedding doesn't have to be over when your reception is over. Kate and Chris wanted to keep the party going after guests were set to leave at 11 p.m., so we rented a private bar for them. We arranged for a DJ to play, and we even had pizza delivered. It's a great idea to arrange for an after party if you want to keep celebrating without ruining the more sophisticated element of your wedding.

FRIDAY NIGHTS

Take a page from Kate's college friends' book, and consider a Friday night wedding, instead of the more traditional Saturday. The couple and their guests made a real vacation out of the weekend, staying at Wild Dunes resort on the Isle of Palms and playing golf on Saturday, before holding a barbecue on Sunday. Reverse the order of things: you'll be more relaxed and apt to catching up with guests once the stress of the big day is over.

PRINTS CHARMING

When it came to envisioning the wedding day photo prints, bride Kate told photographer Liz Banfield to simply "capture the day." Luckily, both were pleased with the final images. Liz offers these tips to find success in hiring the best photographer your money can buy. First, don't assume you can "coach" a photographer into shooting a style that is not represented in his or her portfolio. Second, have a short list of priorities that will help your photographer know how they can both please you and still feel inspired by what's happening. And last, make sure there is plenty of daylight time for ever-flattering natural light shots.

HAPPY ENDINGS

Once the wedding was over, Kate and Chris thought it was about time for Halloween itself to begin! Kate donned a pair of angel wings and Chris—much to the amusement of his bride—dressed up as Spongebob Squarepants. Together with their guests, who had been asked in advance to bring their own costumes, the newlyweds hopped back on the trolleys after the reception and headed to an after party at a local bar.

RIGHT: *Framed in the doorway of the Second Presbyterian Church, the newly married couple stole a kiss.*

exotic india

Rebecca Olson & Dr. Sanjay Gupta

A time-honored Indian wedding ceremony brought

Hindu color and custom to an idyllic Southern setting

for this charismatic television personality who fell

head-over-heels in love with his bride—and the

Charleston lowcountry.

COUPLING

You might have seen Dr. Sanjay Gupta in your living room recently—on television. The practicing neurosurgeon also serves as senior medical correspondent for news network CNN. But when he proposed to attorney Rebecca, after presenting her with a poem he'd written ("I have it framed and still read it every day!" she says.), he was just a love-struck man hoping that his girlfriend would say "yes" to the biggest question he'd ever asked.

The couple met through a mutual pal and remained friends for several years before they started dating. After Sanjay popped the question at Christmas, they had a scant five months to pull a wedding together, because they wanted the weather to still be cool enough for an outdoor ceremony in Charleston. We got to work immediately, creating a beautiful, vibrant occasion that we knew would make the trip down South well worth it for the families and friends of these Michigan natives.

RIGHT: *Eschewing a Western white dress for traditional Hindu garb, Rebecca donned a two-piece lengha, which she had hand-made in India and shipped over just in time for the ceremony. Her wrists were decorated with flower garlands and her hands bore the traditional mendhi designs bestowed on Hindu women before their wedding day.*

SETTING THE SCENE: DESIGN & DÉCOR

Rebecca and Sanjay decided right away that they wanted a traditional Hindu ceremony to honor Sanjay's heritage, which meant I had to brush up on my knowledge of Indian customs! At the same time, they were keen to focus on the beauty of Charleston, so we needed to work some Southern charm in there too. We chose the McBee House at Ashley Hall School as a location.

Besides finding a white horse for Sanjay to ride in on during the baraat—the wedding procession of the groom—our largest task was constructing a mandap, which is the wooden structure under which a Hindu ceremony takes place. We kept it relatively simple, so as not to block the view of the guests as they watched Rama Madugula, the couple's pundit (wedding officiant) perform the ceremony in both English and Sanskrit. We edged it in flowers and fabric and raised it onto a stage, which we covered in seagrass carpeting and trimmed with more fabric.

Our color palette was founded on reds and golds, with splashes of deep purples, blues, and oranges. We borrowed several classic Hindu statues from a local shop owned by friends of Sanjay's parents, which we used to line the aisle; custom dictated that it was imperative that we also find one of Ganesh, the elephant-headed god. For dinner, which we held in a tent on the lawn, we covered tables in rich floor-length bengaline linens in red and orange and used gold pots filled with red roses and tall blue delphinium as centerpieces. I found some Indian-patterned lanterns, which I hung from the trees outside the tent.

SOIRÉE STEP BY STEP:

BUILDING A MANDAP

YOU WILL NEED:

Tent frame only (Order from your local rental company without the top)
Fabric
Scissors
Zip ties or pins to secure fabric
Small stage for underneath tent (order from your local rental company)
Carpet or seagrass to cover your stage
Staple gun

- You can create a mandap from a basic tent frame; a 10 x 10-foot tent should leave you ample room. Set up a small stage underneath your tent, just enough to cover the base of your tent. You can use carpet, or seagrass, to cover the staging pieces. We used seagrass for ours.

- Once the frame has been properly set up by your local tent or rental company, cover the poles in fabric.

- To hide the legs of the stage and the underneath area, you can use matching fabric to create a skirt. Staple the fabric on top of the staging.

- Use zip ties or pins to secure the fabric around the poles. (Zip ties will be more secure and you can fold the fabric back over them if you want to cover them up.)

- After your frame has been covered, you can hang something from the center or create your own top out of your fabric.

SIGNATURE ELEMENTS

ARM CANDY

Rebecca had her traditional lengha (two-piece dress) made in India, though she chose to cut the sleeves off because of the warmer weather. As a surprise, we took the excess material and had a seamstress make her a matching purse, which she carried all evening—and which she'll be able to use in the future to remind her of her wedding day.

COMING UP ROSES

We fashioned our aisle entirely from red rose petals, scattering them in a thick path down the lawn towards the mandap. Inside it, we had several large bowls of loose rose petals, which were sprinkled over the couple at the end, in a gesture thought to ward off evil. In the hands of our gold statues, which guarded the aisle on both sides, we placed lush bunches of the same roses for continuity.

BOTANICAL GARLANDS

As part of the Hindu ceremony, the couple placed fresh flower garlands around each other's necks as a gesture of acceptance and respect. We hand-made red-and-white garlands from roses and orchids, and even did a few shorter ones for Rebecca's wrists. They looked so beautiful against the henna designs—known as mehendi—on her hands.

TAKE A SEAT

Because the mandap is the focal point of the ceremony—the groom's parents traditionally sit on the left and the bride's parents on the right, with the couple in the middle—we wanted to do attractive seating within. We built square-shaped ottomans and covered them with bright orange and red fabric. Then we topped each with a pillow; the ceremony is often lengthy, so we wanted everyone to be comfortable!

ALL IN THE DETAILS

We added plenty of ethnic-inspired touches to the reception, like huge floor pillows in vibrant silks scattered about so people could relax in between dancing to Indian music, which was spun by Sanjay's friend, a DJ. We put Indian silk shades on the existing lamp sconces in the ballroom to create a more Eastern ambiance, and we stuck sparklers into big bowls of rice at the end for the send-off.

LEFT: *The trees surrounding the reception site were lit up with hanging lanterns containing candles that spilled a soft glow through the branches. At the corners of each, delicate hand-strung flower garlands swayed gently in the breeze.* OPPOSITE: *Under swags of richly hued materials, guests enjoyed a family-style sit-down dinner.*

SOIRÉE SECRETS

CEREMONY SEATING

Think outside the box—or rather outside the straight lines—when it comes to arranging the seating for an outdoor ceremony. We organized our chairs around three sides of the mandap, in four separate sets that formed a looping U-shape. It made guests feel less like an impassive audience and more involved in the ceremony—plus everyone got a slightly different view.

ORCHID GARLAND

If you want to decorate with flower garlands, you don't have to order expensive fresh petals or use faux flowers to save money. If you've got a needle and thread—and a steady hand!—it's incredibly easy to make your own. We strung delicate purple and white orchids on fishing line, knotted each one, and hung them from the sides of the mandap and on the lanterns.

TENT DECOR

A less costly route to lining an entire tent is to use swags of several different materials instead; it creates a billowing canopy effect that looks especially pretty when lit up with hanging lamps. Since we had several signature hues for this occasion, we used a variety of swags in rich reds and oranges, with a few blues and purples thrown in.

FAMILY STYLE

If you're serving your food "family style," consider that you might need a wider table to accommodate the large dishes. Our caterer, j.b.c. catering, came up with an extraordinary mixture of lowcountry and Indian cuisine, but I knew we'd need more space to set down those huge serving vessels once they'd been passed around the guests. So we built special-sized tables, simply by laying a 4 x 8-foot piece of plywood atop a regular eight-foot-long table. Once we covered it with linens, you couldn't tell we'd added an extra bit of width.

PRINTS CHARMING

The invitations, menu cards, and favor boxes—filled by Sanjay's family with nuts and raisins—were ordered from India; a deep red with gold print, they were embellished with the "Om" symbol. The gold scrollwork that graced our invitations made an appearance several months later—looping across the buttercream frosting on the five-tier wedding cake, which was sprinkled with edible rose petals.

HAPPY ENDINGS

One of the reasons Sanjay and Rebecca chose such a central, downtown location was so that their guests could easily get back to their hotel rooms afterwards. As for the happy couple themselves, they decided to forgo a getaway car in favor of a Charleston rickshaw pedicab decorated with a few simple rose blooms and the requisite "Just Married" sign. Since rickshaws are also common on the streets of India, it was a pretty fitting way to say goodbye!

RIGHT: *Fresh flowers decorated both the happy couple and their chosen mode of transportation as they left the reception in style aboard a rickshaw.*

Just Married

nature's whimsy

Karly Cammerer & Judd Depew

The bride's love of texture—and her inordinate talent

as a graphic designer—set the pace for this playful,

non-traditional wedding, with a vivid yet natural color

palette taken straight from the great outdoors.

COUPLING

Karly and Judd were introduced in college during her freshman year. She's a native of Ohio and he's from Cape Cod. Oddly enough, they met on a blind date, which is how Karly's parents met as well. They dated for six years before Judd proposed, but not before he'd had a chance to fly back to Ohio—they were both living in Boston at the time—to ask Karly's father for permission. He even disguised his mission by telling her it was purely a business trip!

Judd had his top-secret proposal plan all worked out. The two were heading off on a romantic weekend at the Wauwinet in Nantucket, which, according to Karly, she was on the verge of canceling because she was so busy at work. Judd persuaded her not to, and the pair arrived at the inn as scheduled, only to be told that the toilet was broken in their room, so they wouldn't be able to check in. As compensation, they were offered a free picnic lunch on the beach. Mildly perturbed, Karly agreed and was surprised to find that the picnic contained all her favorite foods. The even bigger surprise, however, came when Judd popped the question! He'd planned the whole thing and got the hotel staff in on it; needless to say, the broken toilet was merely a ruse. As icing on the cake, he'd even had one of Karly's dresses shipped to the inn so she'd have something to wear that evening over a celebratory candlelit dinner. Talk about getting your priorities right!

RIGHT: *Taken straight from nature, the greens, yellows, and oranges of the theme married perfectly with the tranquil surroundings of the River Course at Kiawah Island.* OPPOSITE, ABOVE: *Karly carried a bouquet of snowberries and Star of Bethlehem. Rather than the orange dahlias that made an appearance throughout the wedding, she opted for clean white ones.* OPPOSITE, BELOW: *Walnut wood backing on the envelopes of the invitations provided one of the many inspirations for the wedding. Karly loves working woods and grasses into her designs.*

FAREWELL *brunch*

REHEARSAL
DINNER

Dick and Katy Depew

invite you

to a seaside barbeque

in honor of

Judd and Karly

ABOVE, LEFT: *Mossy green tablecloths in velvet brought nature indoors; orange mums lined the center of the table, the larger vases filled with nests of curly willow.* ABOVE, RIGHT: *Karly's colorful, fanciful designs graced the invitations for the rehearsal dinner and the farewell luncheon. In fact, so impressed was Paper Source, the company who she had print them, that they offered her a job!*

SETTING THE SCENE: DESIGN & DÉCOR

Karly was incredibly fun to work with, because she was very creative; as a graphic designer, she already had many ideas about what she wanted. She chose Soirée, she says, because she saw one of our weddings in a magazine and immediately knew that our style would mesh with hers. When we first met, she'd already designed her own invitations: they were non-traditional and contemporary, with a lot of texture-driven elements and a slight retro, '50s feel. Her tastes were so obvious from her work that we were able to take one look at what she'd drawn up and design her wedding around that.

The ceremony and reception were both held at the River Course on Kiawah Island. Karly grew up summering on the island, and her aunt and uncle have a house there, so we wanted to go with a very outdoorsy feel, incorporating the colors of our natural environment—rich greens and browns and oranges. Because she wanted to stay away from roses and anything too traditional, we used bright orange dahlias everywhere, tying them to the backs of chairs as pew markers, scattering them along the aisle, and, of course, incorporating them into the bouquets and boutonnieres. We brought the same oranges and greens into the reception. Alongside the dining room, we erected a tent—custom-lined with a sheer green fabric with orange and chocolate edging—under which we constructed a hip lounge area, which had a sleek, almost Brat Pack–era feel to it.

SOIRÉE STEP BY STEP:
ICE CREAM BAR & TABLE

YOU WILL NEED:

4 pieces of 1 x 4-foot wood
1 large piece of 3/4-inch-thick plywood
Screws
Paint & paintbrush
Drill
Rubber hose
Bucket for drainage
Water sealant
Lots of crushed ice!
Whatever you choose to put inside: ice blocks, alcohol, etc.

- Bear in mind that this table will be able to sit on standard rental tables; the one we created was fit for a six foot table. Using the 1 x 4-foot pieces of wood for your sides and the piece of plywood for your bottom, determine your box size and screw the pieces together.

- Once you have built your box, use a water sealant on the inside to prevent any leakage through the cracks in the edges.

- Paint the sides of your box your desired color. We like black because it can handle a significant amount of wear and tear without touch-ups!

- Drill a small hole in the bottom to allow for drainage with the hose. (We drilled a hole in the table as well. Be sure to check with your rental company beforehand!)

- Place the box on the table and guide the hose into a bucket underneath for drainage.

- To hide the bottom of the table and whatever is underneath it, you can either staple fabric around the edges and cover your staples with a thick piece of ribbon or you can place a linen on top of your table before you place the box on top.

- Fill the box with lots of crushed ice and whatever your display item is! We've done ice cream in custom cut blocks and an ouzo bar, though you could also do a gazpacho shot station or a vodka bar.

SIGNATURE ELEMENTS

NICE TOUCH

Karly loves playing with texture, so we made sure that while everything was very pleasing to the eye, it was also very pleasing to the touch—a real combination of very different textures and surfaces. We used a mossy green velvet for all the linens, and we had sea grass carpeting in our lounge, along with low leather ottomans and sofas covered with silk and velvet pillows.

NESTING INSTINCTS

We thought it would be a sweet idea for the couple's ring bearer to carry a little bird's nest instead of a ring pillow; it complemented the natural, outdoorsy feel of the wedding. To continue the same theme, we brought a similar element into the reception, by creating a nest of curly willow in square glass vases, which we then topped with orange dahlias. It just added something extra to a centerpiece that could have been very basic.

FLAG DAY

Our signature Lowcountry Lemonade made an appearance at this wedding, but instead of placing a fresh bloom inside the glass, as we often do, we added a novel twist. We fashioned a little flag-cum-swizzle stick by attaching a white rectangle of paper to a wooden dowel and glue-gunning a yellow or green mum to it.

OUT ON A LIMB

To present the wonderful butler cards that Karly had designed, we made a "tree" from live branches and hung the cards from each limb. As a surprise, we duplicated the tree idea for the sign-in station. We had little matching cards made, just like the ones she'd designed, and placed them on a table next to an identical tree. Instead of each guest taking down the card with their name on it to find out at which table they were to sit, the process was reversed. You picked up a card, wrote your message to Karly and Judd, and then hung it on the second tree! It made for great synchronicity.

COLOR ME HUNGRY

Because we'd decided to bring the colors from Karly's invitations into all aspects of the décor, we thought, "Why stop with the food?" It was easy to play with those oranges and browns. For one course, we served miniature pumpkins, hollowed out, and filled with pumpkin soup topped with a sage crème fraîche. We made sure that even the couple's favors—bags of caramel popcorn, Karly's favorite snack—didn't deviate from our color palette!

karly AND judd

SOIRÉE SECRETS

ALTAR OPTIONS

When your ceremony is outside, you don't necessarily want to be topping your altar with a large arrangement of flowers—you're always at the mercy of the weather, and a strong gust of wind could cause them to topple over. To be on the safe side, we filled large glass vases with dried green peas and then glue-gunned orange dahlias to the tops to provide a floral element; the weight of the peas helped to hold the tablecloth down and Karly and Judd could rest assured that the vases wouldn't budge in the breeze.

ICE CREAM DISPLAY

Sure, if you're serving ice cream at your reception, you could just place the tubs in a cooler packed with ice, but it isn't the most elegant look in the world. Karly and Judd had their favorite ice cream, a brand called Graeter's, shipped in from her native Ohio. Because it only came in tiny pint size cartons and because, by happy coincidence, the design of the tubs went very well with our color scheme, I wanted to find a great way to display it. I designed a very simple ice sculpture—basically, just hollowed-out blocks of ice—that allowed us to showcase the tubs of ice cream, while still keeping them adequately frozen. It actually became a really cool (pun intended!) focal point at the reception, in a way that a red cooler packed with ice, while functional, just wouldn't have done.

CAKE DESIGN

We always like to match our bride's cake to some element of her wedding—sometimes it's the lace of her dress or the flowers in her bouquet. Karly's printed materials were such a large part of her personality—and, ultimately, the design of our event—that we felt it was only fitting to take the bold, illustrative stars and flowers and polka dots from her designs and replicate them on the cake in bright greens and yellows and reds. It's all about using your personality to distinguish your wedding; this was a whimsical, quirky wedding, and a traditional cake with elaborate scrollwork would have looked at odds with the funky, fun designs Karly created. In short, it likely wouldn't have been very "her."

PRINTS CHARMING

"I know there are many people out there who could walk into a stationery shop and be thrilled to order a black engraved invitation on ecru stock, but I'm definitely not one of them," says Karly. She wanted her printed materials to have "a wow factor," she says, and to introduce an atmosphere where "every guest would feel comfortable, but would still say, 'I've never seen anything like this before!'" In our planning for the wedding, we took the natural-looking greens and oranges from her designs: the walnut wood backing of the invitation envelope was really our starting point for incorporating texture, as well as the piece of leather that tied together her rehearsal dinner invitation.

HAPPY ENDINGS

Because Karly and Judd were married on the River Course, we thought it would be fun to have them leave in a golf cart, which we decked out with mums to match those we'd put in our signature cocktail earlier in the evening. I loved the fact that we ended on a very playful note, because the whole event was very light-hearted and unique and veered quite far from tradition in so many ways.

something blue

Lainey Faulkner & Trip McMahon

Under live oaks in a Lowcountry island paradise, a couple

says "I do" to a North-meets-South wedding, with a

formal setting and the soul of old-fashioned sweetness.

COUPLING

A vacation in Chicago is nothing to sniff at, of course, and that's what Philadelphia native Lainey Faulkner thought she was getting until, as they stood in line at the airport, boyfriend Trip McMahon pulled out two tickets—to Paris. The college sweethearts, who met during the first week of Lainey's junior year, set off for a whirlwind week of romance—and still, says Lainey, she had no idea that a second surprise was right around the corner.

Recalling their second day in the City of Light, Lainey says, "We got a little lost and just walked and walked and walked around Paris. It was so perfect. On the way home, it started raining, and just as we were crossing over the Seine, Trip stopped and asked me to marry him." The two decided on lowcountry haven Spring Island, where Trip's parents have a house, as their dream location. "We're both from different cities," says Lainey, " so we thought that as long as our friends and relatives were coming such a long way for our wedding, why not make it a real vacation?"

RIGHT: *Inspired by a vintage-looking floral design, which made frequent appearances throughout the wedding, creamy blue-and-white letterpressed invitations cut a dashing figure when they arrived on the doorsteps of guests.*
OPPOSITE: *The addition of blueberries to the mouth-watering cake—inspired both by the lace of Lainey's dress and the patterns on the invitation—added a little of the signature color into even the most unlikely of places.*

MR. AND MRS. JOSEPH FAULKNER
REQUEST THE HONOUR OF YOUR PRESENCE
AT THE MARRIAGE OF THEIR DAUGHTER

elaine kathryn

TO

william coulson mcmahon III

SATURDAY, THE TENTH OF JUNE
TWO THOUSAND AND SIX
AT HALF PAST FIVE O'CLOCK IN THE EVENING

OLD TABBY RUINS
SPRING ISLAND, SOUTH CAROLINA

Dinner and dancing immediately following the ceremony

ABOVE, LEFT: *White leather chaises made a quirky but stunning addition to the lounge tent, giving a smooth, modern feel to a space that could have become stuffy.* ABOVE, RIGHT: *Custom-lined with sheer blue chiffon that hung in folded pleats from the ceiling, the tent boasted indoor features like carpet, chandeliers, and curtains, which blew prettily in the breeze.*

SETTING THE SCENE: DESIGN & DÉCOR

Lainey hadn't decided on a color scheme when we first met, but shortly afterwards she was looking for bridesmaid dresses in Trip's hometown of Chicago and some gorgeous silvery-blue gowns caught her eye. They looked divine on the girls, so we decided to go with blue for the entire wedding, pairing it with white for a simple, timeless look. Lainey was drawn to vintage-inspired elements—the prints on her invitations, for example, and antique-looking china—and she wanted to create a fairly formal feel, with touches like silver-footed bowls. When designing that kind of look, though, the key is not to let "dressy" verge into "stuffy," and this we remedied by incorporating a few contemporary elements, which was a little unexpected but brought a certain modernity to the space.

After the ceremony at the Old Tabby Ruins—the old plantation house on Spring Island—guests headed over to the Golf House for cocktails, dinner, and dancing in the tent we'd custom-lined with sheer ice blue chiffon. A chandelier hung over each table, which were set with blue and silver satin linens with piping edges and inverted pleats to match the edging of the tent. Each centerpiece was made up of peonies, gardenias, and Cattleya orchids, to echo the flowers Lainey had carried down the aisle, and we had vases of bright blue hydrangeas interspersed around the room for impact. The mood was refined and genteel, ensuring a proper Southern welcome for the out-of-town couple and their guests.

SOIRÉE STEP BY STEP:

DRINK UMBRELLAS AND ROSE PETAL BOXES

YOU WILL NEED:

Paper printed with your design of choice
Wooden skewers
Rose petals
Ribbon

For the drink umbrellas:

- Cut your paper into 2.5 x 2.5-inch squares.

- Fold them to create an umbrella shape, poke a small hole through them with the skewer, and place them in your drinks.

For the rose petal boxes:

- Visit your local crafts store to learn about origami boxes and find the right style for you. Create your box from instructions.

- Fill it with rose petals and tie it with a ribbon to finish.

SIGNATURE ELEMENTS

THE CONSTANT GARDENIA

There's nothing more exquisite than the smell of gardenias on a balmy June night, and we took full advantage of that! For the ceremony, we fashioned balls made of the buds and hung them with blue silk ribbon on wrought iron hooks down the sides of the aisle. At the butler card table, an individual shallow silver bowl containing a single gardenia greeted each guest, propping up the card bearing their name.

THE PLEAT GOES ON

To match the sheer blue chiffon on the inside of the tent, we covered the base of our bar with the same fabric, affixing it so that it fell in the same gentle, folded pleats lining the ceiling. Matching the fabrics not only lent a certain uniformity to the space but also gave that sense of seeing something slightly unexpected but familiar.

SWEET STUFF

Lainey's gown was stunning: a solid lace that just begged to be incorporated somewhere into the wedding. Cake designer Jim Smeal decorated each alternating layer of her gorgeous confection—which was silvery-blue with white piping—with the lace pattern on her gown.

A SENSE OF PLACE

At a sit-down dinner, numbered tables are indispensable—but "Table 4" hardly glows with personality, does it? The couple decided to have a little fun with labeling the tables, and instead of using numbers, named each one after a street significant to them: the one on which Trip proposed, for example, and the place Lainey's grandparents had lived. As well as adding a bit of a spark to an otherwise mundane reception element, the named tables served as conversation starters for guests. "Which city is our table in, do you think?" is a little peppier than, "And how do you know the bride?"

GIVE AND RECEIVE

Guests were certainly ready for their close-up at this wedding; as well as saying "cheese" for the Polaroid sign-in station, we had them take a second picture of themselves, and this we used for a different purpose. Lainey's brother has Downs Syndrome, and she and Trip decided that rather than give guests a favor, they'd make a donation to the school he attends. While the guests' hearts were undoubtedly full with this knowledge, the couple didn't want them leaving empty-handed; thus, we created cards that said "In Lieu Of Favors," to which each guest affixed the picture they'd taken as a keepsake.

LEFT: *Welcoming their guests to Spring Island, Lainey and Trip had simple, comprehensive, yet graceful booklets made by The Lettered Olive to match their other printed materials.* OPPOSITE, RIGHT: *Propped up by a gardenia resting in a silver bowl, handwritten cards inscribed with each guest's name let them know which table to head to for supper.*

WELCOME
TO SPRING ISLAND!
LOVE, LAINEY AND TRIP

SOIRÉE SECRETS

CLEAN LOOK

Hiding all your hardware and wires is the secret to a streamlined look—and you can even do it while simultaneously enhancing the décor. We wrapped the chains hanging our chandeliers with the same ice blue fabric we'd used elsewhere, disguising the out-of-place chains with a smoother look. To hide the ugly stage equipment, we placed a row of boxwood trees at the edge of the dance floor and strung them with lights. Not only did we disguise wires, but we even lit up the dance floor a little more!

SWEETHEART TABLE

Chances are you won't have had a moment alone with your new husband since the brief few seconds when you walked down the aisle together, and the two of you certainly have a lot to talk about! Consider what's known as a Sweetheart Table—a private table for two for you and your beau, far from the maddening crowd of long-lost aunts and uncles all desperate to grab you and chat. This way, you can catch up with your new spouse, enjoy your dinner without answering a dozen questions between mouthfuls, and then get up and make the rounds without feeling rude for leaving other guests at the table.

COLORFUL FOOD

Although the idea of blue food might bring to mind unappealing images of additive-laden junk, take comfort in the fact that you can still bring your color scheme into your menu without insisting your guests sip bright blue Slushies for dessert. Because it was a summer wedding and blueberries were in season, we incorporated the fruit into Lainey's cake; you couldn't see it from the outside, but when the slices were cut, the perfect berries were visible on the inside, adding a unique design element to the cake as much as an extra burst of flavor.

GUEST BAGS

Guest bags monogrammed with the bride and groom's names and wedding date might be a cute idea, but consider their longevity; will your old college roommate want to carry around a bag with someone else's initials on it. Rather than having Lainey's and Trip's names embroidered onto our guest bags, we chose the Spring Island Club logo instead; it was subtle enough to encourage guests to reuse the bag once they got back to their old lives but still ensured that they'd never forget the wonderful weekend they spent on Spring Island.

PRINTS CHARMING

The Lettered Olive designed all of our printed materials, from the save-the-date cards to the display tags on the groomsmen's boutonniere boxes. We used a cream card with silvery-blue calligraphy and made sure the familiar vintage-looking flower pattern that Lainey loved made frequent appearances. For the ceremony programs and menus, we added a silvery-blue ribbon for a little extra elegance. Even the design around the edges of the china at dinner was similar to the pattern on our printed materials, which was certainly a happy coincidence! The champagne glasses had a similar etching as well.

HAPPY ENDINGS

It was sweet and fitting for Lainey and Trip to leave on a golf cart after they'd been married at the Spring Island Club. We decorated it with the requisite "Just Married" sign, complete with the familiar flower pattern, and we hung the gardenia balls we'd used in the ceremony with blue satin ribbon. Lainey told me that for the rest of her life, every time she smells gardenias she'll remember her wedding night and riding away at the end of the reception so incredibly happy.

RIGHT: *Spring Island, close to Beaufort, South Carolina, made the perfect backdrop for Lainey and Trip's big day.*

rain or shine

Sarah Steele & Jason Barclay

A last-minute location change and a mid-afternoon rainstorm didn't prevent this beautiful flower-filled wedding from wowing guests with a myriad of signature touches.

COUPLING

Sarah and Jason are both from Indiana, and they met there while they were working on a campaign for the state governor. The funny thing is, though, they found out later that they'd attended the University of Virginia at the same time and even lived in the same apartment complex without their paths ever crossing!

Jason knew that Sarah loved tulips—he'd often surprise her with a bunch during their courtship—so when he decided to propose, he led her on a scavenger hunt through her house, presenting her with a note in each room which detailed a special moment from their year together. Finally, he led her into the last room, where he'd had a hundred tulips delivered, and asked if she'd do him the honor of marrying him. It just so happened that they had a trip to Charleston planned shortly afterwards; they fell in love with the city and, with weddings on the brain, decided to hold the ceremony there.

RIGHT: *Shortly after he'd said his vows, Jason kept true to his word to love, honor, comfort, and keep his new wife by gallantly protecting her from the rain.* OPPOSITE, ABOVE: *Both of Jason's younger sisters served as flower girls, carrying square boxes covered in bright pink ranunculuses instead of the more traditional baskets.* OPPOSITE, BELOW: *The wedding cake shared by Sarah and Jason was miniature as well—though it was slightly bigger than those given to each guest—so they could save the top for their anniversary.*

SETTING THE SCENE: DESIGN & DÉCOR

After Sarah told me how Jason had proposed, I knew we had to make tulips a large part of the wedding. She has a very casual, laid-back style, although she's also very sophisticated, and we wanted the wedding to reflect that combination. We went with a base of greens, which were very fresh and crisp and spring-like—and added a few pink accents, primarily in our flowers.

The ceremony was set to take place at the Confederate Home and Garden, but sheets of rain started coming down during the afternoon, and the minister who was marrying the two kindly offered the First Baptist Church as an alternate location. We had to think on our feet with the décor, as we hadn't anticipated a church wedding. In the end we kept it simple, scattering green orchids on either side of the aisle and filling a huge urn with an enormous arrangement of tulips at the altar.

For our reception at the Gibbes Museum of Art, guests kept dry under a clear-top tent with swags of sheer green taffeta looping down from the ceiling. Sarah and Jason wanted a sit-down dinner, so we had square tables with bamboo-style chairs, topped with green bengaline linen and edged in green taffeta with inverted pleats and green piping. Our centerpieces were simple: low arrangements of pink peonies, orchids, and tulips in clear glass vases. We built a long wooden bar for guests to sit at—the bar stools matched the chairs—and created a lounge area with green taffeta ottomans and white sofas topped with green-and-white striped pillows.

SOIRÉE STEP BY STEP:
HANGING CANDLE ARRANGEMENTS

YOU WILL NEED:

1 x 2-foot wood (for edging)
3/4-inch-thick plywood
Paint and paintbrush
Screws
Wire (strong enough to hang)
Gorilla Glue (or other wood glue)

- Determine the size of your arrangements.

- Cut the 3/4-inch-thick plywood piece to the appropriate size. Use the 1 x 2s to create a "lip" around the edges of your plywood piece and screw into place. To secure the edge further, use Gorilla Glue or other wood glue before the edges are attached. (You don't want anything to fall out of your arrangement once it is hanging.)

- Paint your arrangement box entirely.

- Drill holes or a slit in the middle of all four sides. (The size of these will depend on how big your box is and how thick your ribbon is for hanging.)

- Run two long pieces of ribbon through the slits just like you were wrapping a present. (We used thick double-sided satin ribbon.) The ribbon should show underneath your box as a cross, and you can also attach eyelets or use wire again depending on the size of your arrangement and what you are planning to hang.

- Hang your arrangement in place and decorate with a floral piece or use glass cylinders with candles to create an interesting lighting effect.

THE WEDDING OF
sarah AND jason

SIGNATURE ELEMENTS

TRUE ROMANCE

We got a little creative with the lighting for this wedding reception: rather than chandeliers or paper lanterns, we lit the entire tent with candles. I built wooden platforms to hang over the tables and the bar; they each held four glass cylinders containing ivory candles and were hung from the ceiling with ribbon. I took the same idea and built a large-scale version to hang over the dance floor. Honestly, is there anything more romantic than a whole room lit by candles?

GORGEOUS GREETINGS

As an alternative to a floral wreath, we filled antique wrought-iron flower baskets with an abundance of pink, green, and white flowers; they were just spilling out of the basket, and it looked gorgeous. The baskets were hung on the gates of the church and the Gibbes Museum, welcoming guests to Sarah and Jason's wedding.

SHELF AWARE

In our quest for a candlelit glow, we rented several sets of bookcases and placed them behind the long wooden bar we'd built. On the lower shelves, we put the spare glassware so the bartender would have easy access to it, but the higher shelves we lined with glass votives holding tiny white candles. Guests had something pretty to look at, and we managed to light the room with a natural glow.

BUDDING IDEAS

Our seating assignment table doubled as our sign-in; we had a Polaroid station set up, because people just love having pictures from the wedding on the same night! We filled glass cylinders with orchids, then attached butler cards to skewers and placed them in each vase. It looked so elegant and original.

YOU CAN TAKE IT WITH YOU

On the back of each chair, we had little empty take-home boxes that doubled as place cards, saying "Sarah and Jason" and a tag with each guest's name. Each box had "Have your cake and eat it too" written on the tag, urging guests to take their leftovers home with them. It was a huge hit—I don't think a single person left the reception without a slice of cake in their little box!

SERVICE WITH A SURPRISE

Steamed lobster wontons were presented in individual bamboo baskets. It was actually a very sweet surprise for Sarah; they were one of the things she and I agreed we had to take out once we realized we were over budget. The chef hated to see her disappointed, so he surprised her with them. She was over the moon!

Dinner and Dancing

IMMEDIATELY FOLLOWING THE CEREMONY

THE GIBBES MUSEUM OF ART

CHARLESTON, SOUTH CAROLINA

LEFT: *The large party table was a big hit; guests were able to sit between dances and catch up.* OPPOSITE, LEFT: *Moss green mesh guest bags held bottled water, pralines, a guest booklet, and a copy of the local classic,* Mrs. Whaley and Her Charleston Garden. OPPOSITE, RIGHT: *Soirée employee Lexi made sure Sarah and Jason stayed dry.*

SOIRÉE SECRETS

CHANGING PLACES

Great service is the key to handling problems that pop up unexpectedly. When we had to change the ceremony location at the last minute, it was my staff at Soirée who made it seem like less of a problem to the poor bride who was fretting about the rain. We directed our trolley drivers to take guests to the First Baptist Church instead of the Confederate Home & College, and we had someone waiting at the latter to redirect those who might have ventured there on their own. We had a huge stockpile of big white golf umbrellas on hand, so no one ruined their hair, their dress, or their shoes, and we were out on the dance floor, mopping it between every song so no one slipped and fell. We made the best of the situation, trying to handle every potential issue that cropped up because of the rain—and we made sure that the guests had an absolute blast regardless.

COMFORT FOR GUESTS

At a destination wedding, when the closest thing most guests have to familiarity is their hotel room, it's a nice idea to make them feel as comfortable and at-home as you can, even while they're out of town. Sarah specified to me that she didn't want a wedding that felt "uppity;" it was important to her that people felt able to relax. As such, I wanted to create an area in the lounge where guests could gather around a large, homey table, like they were in their kitchen or family room at home. We placed a large 8 x 8-foot square board atop a smaller table, covered the whole thing with fabric, candles, and flowers, and edged it with banquet seating. The result? A big party table where everyone could congregate and catch up.

CREATING CURTAINS

You can hide pretty much everything with enough fabric. I wanted to set up a little porch area off the tent, in front of a large pair of doors leading into the museum. But the last thing I wanted was for it to look like I'd just shoved a couch and some tables in front of some doors, so we made a fantastic backdrop by hanging a fabric curtain over a wooden frame. We placed a couple of banquettes and ottomans in front of the curtain and added a side table with a reading lamp and a vase of flowers to give it a relaxed, homey feel. The backdrop of material warmed up the space and gave a cozy but uniform look, tying the rest of the décor into the area.

PRINTS CHARMING

The Lettered Olive designed every aspect of Sarah's printed materials so that everything matched—from the sign on the floral welcome baskets to the ceremony programs to the stickers on the take-away boxes. We sent Sarah a few samples of invitations, and she chose the first one she received, after showing it to her mother who said, "Oh, that's just so you." The look was classic and crisp, with dark green script on a white background and a vintage-inspired tulip design. On the guest bag tags, for example, you can see individual tulip buds, while the invitations feature an enlarged leaf curlicue. Everything was uniform, with that same clean green and white design continuing throughout.

HAPPY ENDINGS

It was still sprinkling a little when Sarah and Jason left the reception, but they decided to make a run for it anyway! Sheltered under an umbrella, they made their way to the rickshaw/pedicab we'd decorated with a "Just Married" sign, as guests threw orchids at them. Of her wedding day, Sarah says, "There's nothing about it that I would have done any differently. Every single person who was there has said to me that when they walked into the reception tent for the first time, there was a collective gasp at how beautiful it was. The whole event just couldn't have been any more wonderful."

Some of the Soirée staff take a break: Lexi Ritsch, Tara Guérard (holding photographer Liz Banfield's son Grier), Kate Badger Little, Susan Kelly, Tziporah Schwartz, Martha Robbins and Mary Helen Peacock (not pictured Heather Santucci).

wedding resources

ART SUPPLIES

Artist & Craftsman Supply
Charleston, SC
843.579.0077

CALLIGRAPHY

Elizabeth Porcher Jones
Charleston, SC
843.402.0308
www.elizporcher@aol.com

CANDLES, FLORALS, SUPPLIES

Cross Garden Center
Charleston, SC
843.766.1687

Florabundance
Carpinteria, CA
800.201.3597

Horst Wholesale Florist
Charleston, SC
843.556.5151

Hyam's
Charleston, SC
843.795.4570

Mayesh Wholesale
Los Angeles, CA
800.954.2000
www.mayesh.com

Rosebank Farms
Johns Island, SC
843.768.9139

Thackeray Farms
Wadmalaw Island, SC
843.559.9058

Tommy's Wholesale Florist, Inc.
Florence, SC
800.968.8211

CATERING AND BEVERAGES

Ben Arnold Sunbelt-Beverage, Co.
Hanahan, SC
www.benarnold-sunbelt.com

Clarey's Liquor
Charleston, SC
843.884.5218

j.b.c. catering
Charleston, SC
843.971.5215
www.jbccatering.com

Patrick Property Events
Charleston, SC
843.853.1810
www.thewilliamaikenhouse.com

Tidewater Foods & Catering, LLC
Charleston, SC
843.762.9200
www.foodforthesouthernsoul.com

CAKES

Wedding Cakes by Jim Smeal
Charleston, SC
843.795.6114
weddingcakesbyjimsmeal.com

Tiers of Joy
Esthi Steffenelli
Charleston, SC
843.849.9979

DECORATIVE ACCESSORIES

Allison Abney Handbags
Charleston, SC
www.allisonabney.com
Allison@allisonabney.com

Magar Hatworks
Charleston, SC
843.577.7740
www.magarhatworks.com

DÉCOR

Anthropologie
www.anthropologie.com

Carolina Mirrors and Shelving
Charleston, SC
843.720.7182

Christian Carpet & Binding
Charleston, SC
843.556.9568

Continental Home
Bedford, NH
800.343.4030
www.continentalhome.net

Design Ideas
Springfield, IL
800.426.6394
www.designid.com

Dwelling
Charleston, SC
843.723.9699

Elizabeth Stuart Design
Charleston, SC
843.577.6272
www.esdcharleston.com

Hills Imports
Atlanta, GA
770.435.1848

Hue
Portland, ME
207.772.4695

Ice Age/Ice Sculptures
Charleston, SC
843.873.6155
www.iceagesculpture.com

Metal Urges
Carlsbad, CA
760.929.1914

Metropolitan Deluxe
Charleston, SC
843.722.0436

Pearl River
New York, NY
800.878.2446
www.pearlriver.com

Pieces
Atlanta, GA
404.869.2476
www.piecesinc.com

Redux
(custom tent covers)
Charleston, SC
843.345.5049

Robert Kahns Wholesale
Charleston, SC
843.722.7926

Soiree, Inc.
(all custom banquettes, etc.)
Charleston, SC
843.577.5006
www.soireecharleston.com

Solaria Lighting
Atlanta, GA
404.508.1987
www.solaria-home.com

Skinner Associates
Westfield, IN
800.645.2106

Tiger Lily
Charleston, SC
843.723.2808
www.tigerlilyflorist.com

Warwick Silver
Hauppauge, NY
warwicksilver.com

Y Design Custom Lamps
Charleston, SC
843.577.0819

FABRICS/LINENS

Immediate Tablecloth
Belleville, New Jersey
800.524.2588

Resource One
Los Angeles, CA
818.343.3451
www.resourceone.info

Robey's Wholesale Fabrics
Connelly Springs, NC
800.386.0633
www.robeysfabrics.com

Rosebrand
New York, New York
800.223.1624
www.rosebrand.com

Read Brothers, LLC
Charleston, SC
843.723.7276

FAVORS AND PACKAGING

Accent Linens and Embroidery
Pasadena, CA
888.222.1282

A Taste of the South
Columbia, SC
803.772.0940
www.atasteofthesouth.com

Bags and Bows
www.bagsandbowsonline.com

Beautiful Cookies
www.beautifulcookies.com

Bulk Foods
www.bulkfoods.com

Burdick Chocolates
www.burdickchocolates.com

Carolina Plantation Rice
Darlington, SC
877.742.3496
www.carolinaplantationrice.com

Charleston Magazine
www.charlestonmag.com

Dale & Thomas Popcorn
Teaneck, NJ
www.daleandthomaspopcorn.com

Data Imaging
Charleston, SC
843.571.8855
www.datai.com

Finishing Touches, Inc.
Carlsborg, WA
360.681.3876

Kudzu Bakery
Georgetown, SC
843.546.1847

Koch's Bakery
Chattanooga, TN
423-265-3331

Liquid Culture
Charleston, SC
843.554.2370

Market Street Sweets
Charleston, SC
843.722.1397

Monogramming by Margaret & Lil
Lhw1936@aol.com

Olde Colony Bakery
Mt. Pleasant, SC
800.722.9932
www.oldecolonybakery.com

Salem Baking Company
Winston-Salem, NC
336.748.0230
www.salembaking.com

Solebury Soap Company Wholesale
(customized soap)
Columbus, OH
866.398.8554

Peking Handicraft
www.pkhc.com

FLORAL DESIGN

All floral design by Soirée, Inc.
Charleston, SC
843.577.5006
www.soireecharleston.com

LOCATIONS/CHURCHES

Ashley Hall—The McBee House
Charleston, SC
843.722.4088
www.ashleyhall.org

The Confederate Home & College
Charleston, SC
843.722.2026

The Country Club of Charleston
Charleston, SC
843.795.8009

Debordieau Beach Club
Pawleys Island, SC
843.527.6000

Drayton Hall Plantation
Charleston, SC
843.769.2600
www.draytonhall.org

First Baptist Church
Charleston, SC
843.722.3896

First (Scots) Presbyterian Church
Charleston, SC
843.722.8882

The French Huguenot Church
Charleston, SC
www.frenchchurch.org

The Gibbes Museum of Art
Charleston, SC
843.722.2706

The Golf Club at Briar's Creek
John's Island, SC
843.768.3050

Greek Orthodox Church
Charleston, SC
843.577.2063

Hibernian Hall
Charleston, SC
843.722.1463

La Fourchette Restaurant
Charleston, SC
843.722.6261

The River Course
Kiawah Island, SC
843.768.5715
www.kiawahislandclub.com

The Sanctuary Hotel
Kiawah Island, SC
877.683.1234
www.thesanctuary.com

Spring Island Golf House/Tabby Ruins
Spring Island, SC
800.242.8175
www.springisland.com

The William Aiken House
Charleston, SC
843.853.1810
www.williamaikenhouse.com

DC Rental
Washington, DC
703.671.7300
www.dcrental.com

Plants Alive, LLC
Ravenel, SC
843.345.5735

Perfect Settings
Washington, DC
202.722.2900
www.perfectsettings.com

Production Design Associates
Charleston, SC
843.554.3466
www.pdalightingandsound.com

Snyder Event Rentals
3895 Meeting Street
Charleston, SC
843.766.3366
www.snydereventrentals.com

Unique Tabletop Rentals
Alexandria, VA
703.333.3454
www.uniquetabletoprentals.com

PHOTOGRAPHY

Liz Banfield
Minneapolis, MN
612.824.2465
www.lizbanfield.com

Adrienne Page
Saint Paul, MN
612.961.1904
www.adriennepage.com

RIBBON

Midori, Inc.
Seattle, WA
800.659.3049
www.midoriribbon.com

SALON SERVICES

Bellezza Salon and Spa
Charleston, SC
843.573.1112
www.bellezzasalonspa.com

Hair by Juliet Jones
Charleston, SC
843.532.8472
www.hairbyjuliet.com

Kristy McMillan of Landis
Charleston, SC
843.723.6100

Makeup by Kori Mahoney
Gwynn's
Charleston, SC
843.795.4009

PRINTING & PAPERS

Bella Figura
Syracuse, NY
315.473.0933
www.bellafigura.com

Cambridge Essex Stamp Company
Mount Kisco, NY
914.241.8726

Oscar and Emma Design
614.245.0812

Kate's Paperie
New York, NY
www.katespaperie.com

The Lettered Olive
www.theletteredolive.com

Nelson Printing
Charleston, SC
843.723.7233
www.nelsonprint.com

Paper Source
www.paper-source.com

Reaves Engraving
Laurinburg, NC
www.reavesengraving.com
877.610.4499

SAS-E Ink
Charleston, SC
843.577.2774

Waste Not Paper Wholesale
Chicago, IL
800.867.2737
www.wastenotpaper.com

TABLEWARE

Abigails
Alexandria, LA
800.678.8485
www.abigails.net

Jamali Garden
New York, NY
www.jamaligarden.com

TRANSPORTATION

Absolutely Charleston
Charleston, SC
843.884.9505

Charleston Rickshaw Company
Charleston, SC
843.723.5685

Star Limo
Charleston, SC
843.889.8400

WEDDING DRESSES AND CLOTHING

Berlins for Men & Women
Charleston, SC
843.723.5591
www.berlinsclothing.com

Bob Ellis Shoes
Charleston, SC
843.722.2515
www.bobellisshoes.com

Copper Penny
Charleston, SC
843.881.3449
www.shopcopperpenny.com

Grady Ervin & Co.
Charleston, SC
843.722.1776
www.gradyervin.com

*Please note, many of the weddings
pictured in this book were destination
weddings and Soirée, Inc. was not
responsible for the purchase of gowns.*

JEWELER

C. Schomburg & Son
Columbus, GA
706.327.7489

FAVORITE CHARLESTON VENDORS
NOT PICTURED

Access Portable Toilets
www.accessportabletoilets.com

A Charleston Bride
www.acharlestonbride.com

Allen Johnson Ceremony Officiant
allen@meetingstreetinn.com

Amey Warder Photography
ameywarder@aol.com

Archer Music Service, LLC
www.archermusic.com

Artistic Eye Productions
www.artisticeyeproductions.com

Bill Struhs Photography
843.722.0230

Carolina Catering
www.carolinacaters.com

Celeste Joye Photography
www.joyephotography.com

Chapel Street Players—Robbi Kenney
stringmusic@onebox.com

Charleston Bay Gourmet Catering
www.charlestonbaygourmet.com

Charleston Outdoor Catering
843.769.6889

Charleston Place Hotel
www.charlestonplace.com

Cru Café
www.crucafe.com

David Edwards Photography
www.dpestudios.com

Distinctive Events—Tally Angle
843.795.6114
www.distinctive-events.com

Earthling Day Spa
www.earthlingdayspa.com

East Coast Entertainment
www.eastcoastentertainment.com

Fat Cat Productions
www.fatcatproductions.com

GDC
www.gdchome.com

Good Food Catering
www.goodfoodcatering.net

Hamby Catering
www.cateringtocharleston.com

Honey Dew Day Spa
www.honeydewdayspa.com

Island Shuttles
www.islandshuttle.com

Lori Lethco Ceremony Coordinator
lori@fbcharleston.org

Marni Rothschild Photography
www.marnipictures.com

Mediterra Catering
www.mediterracatering.com

Nature's Calling, Inc.
www.naturescallinginc.com

On the Market Tours
www.onthemarkettours.com

Palmetto Carriage Company
www.carriagetour.com

Peninsula Grill
www.peninsulagrill.com

Renaissance Weddings
www.renaissancemedia.net

Sam Hill Entertainment
www.samhillbands.com

South Carolina Society Hall
843.723.9032

Security
Kenneth Barfield
Kevin Boyd
843.973.4860

Stella Nova Spa and Salon
www.stella-nova.com

Sublime Pies & Cakes
843.225.5463

Sunbelt Rentals
www.sunbeltrentals.com

Susan Dunn Ceremony Officiant
SKINGDUNN@aol.com

Taylor Stewart Photography
www.taylorstewartphotography.com

Vieuxtemps
www.vieuxtemps.net

Weddings Elegantly Designed
www.charlestonevent.com

Wentworth Mansion
www.wentworthmansion.com

The Wickliffe House
www.wickliffehouse.com

The Willis Blume Agency
www.willisblume.com

Yeehaw Junction
www.yeehawjunction.net

Soirée Inc. by Tara Guérard coordinates, plans, and designs weddings and events, with offices in Charleston, South Carolina. Available for travel. Tara can be contacted at 843.577.5006 or www.soireecharleston.com. Our sister company, The Lettered Olive creates custom stationery suites for all occasions. For more information, contact the Soirée office or visit www.theletteredolive.com.